T0329397

CAMBRIDGE CLASSICAL STUDIES

General Editors

F. M. CORNFORD, D. S. ROBERTSON, F. E. ADCOCK

THE THEORY OF MOTION IN
PLATO'S LATER DIALOGUES

THE THEORY OF MOTION
IN
PLATO'S LATER DIALOGUES

BY

J. B. SKEMP, M.A.
Fellow of Gonville and Caius College

CAMBRIDGE
AT THE UNIVERSITY PRESS
1942

CAMBRIDGE UNIVERSITY PRESS
Cambridge, New York, Melbourne, Madrid, Cape Town,
Singapore, São Paulo, Delhi, Mexico City

Cambridge University Press
The Edinburgh Building, Cambridge CB2 8RU, UK

Published in the United States of America by Cambridge University Press, New York

www.cambridge.org
Information on this title: www.cambridge.org/9781107699182

© Cambridge University Press 1942

This publication is in copyright. Subject to statutory exception
and to the provisions of relevant collective licensing agreements,
no reproduction of any part may take place without the written
permission of Cambridge University Press.

First published 1942
First paperback edition 2013

A catalogue record for this publication is available from the British Library

ISBN 978-1-107-69918-2 Paperback

Cambridge University Press has no responsibility for the persistence or
accuracy of URLs for external or third-party internet websites referred to in
this publication, and does not guarantee that any content on such websites is,
or will remain, accurate or appropriate.

CONTENTS

CONTENTS

PREFACE

The present essay is an enlargement and a revised presentation of work begun in Edinburgh in 1935 under the supervision of Professor A. E. Taylor.

The original thesis was submitted by the writer to his College in the autumn of 1936. Since that date Professor Cornford's interpretations of the *Timaeus* and of the *Parmenides* have appeared. The writer has had these works before him and has had the privilege of discussing the questions at issue with Professor Cornford personally. The essay as it now stands may seem to take account of the work of these two great scholars rather too exclusively, but it must be remembered that anyone who writes in our day on questions connected with the *Timaeus* can hardly do otherwise; nor would anyone who has worked under both of them wish to do otherwise.

Plato's Cosmology challenges assent or disagreement with the main principle of interpretation of the *Timaeus* which Professor Cornford adopts—that it is seriously intended by Plato as a setting forth of his own cosmological ideas with only the necessary minimum of fidelity to the dramatic setting. The writer assents. In his original thesis he stated a case against Professor Taylor's view of the dialogue. It is not restated in the present essay except by implication. This does not imply, however, an unconsidered rejection of all these arguments, still less any lack of appreciation of the help and encouragement he has received from Professor Taylor himself.

A deliberate exclusion of Stoic, neo-Platonist, Christian Platonist and Scholastic terms from a discussion of Plato's dialogues may need defence. Some will even suggest that a failure to relate one's findings to modern philosophical and scientific developments is reprehensible. No defence can be attempted here. The attempt to place the dialogues in the context of ancient thought and life and to lay stress on Plato's debt to the pre-Socratics may be trusted to offer some compensation for the other deficiencies.

I am most grateful to the Rev. C. F. Angus, of Trinity Hall, for much helpful discussion and criticism and to my friends, Dr Helene Weiss and the Rev. J. N. Sanders, for reading the proofs of this essay and finally to the Readers of the University Press for their courtesy and patience.

J. B. S.

Gonville and Caius College
February 1942

INTRODUCTION

A turning-point in the history of human thought was reached when Plato achieved in his doctrine of Forms a synthesis between Hellenic rationalism and Oriental mysticism. No interpretation of Plato can be adequate which fails to do justice to both these elements. His double outlook is revealed at once in the elementary observation that the abstract argument of the dialogues is relieved here and there by a piece of myth the material for which is drawn from current religious conceptions.

NYGREN, Eros and Agape,
tr. Fr. A. G. HEBERT

We are not concerned to enquire how far Plato's employment of the doctrine of Forms shows a "synthesis between Hellenic rationalism and Oriental mysticism". We have rather to discover whether it is fair to regard this doctrine as the only "abstract argument" (which means presumably the only serious metaphysic) in Plato's dialogues and the rest as myth brought in to relieve the strain. Nygren's comment is interesting because it is a typical modern continental view. The Marburg school taught, in essence, that the Forms-doctrine incorporates all that is truly philosophical in Plato, and the various Hegelian interpretations have fortified this position. The Pythagorean mathematical approach of M. Robin and Mr Hardie's[1] recent neo-Platonic interpretation may be said to agree in this, for Mr Hardie is concerned to find the One in Plato's *Parmenides*, not to ask how far Plotinus's teaching on nature and emanation builds on bases Plato had prepared. This axiom that Forms-doctrine and metaphysic are co-extensive for Plato is denied by the two great English commentators whose work on the later dialogues has been published since the end of the last war. Taylor and Cornford differ on so many points that their agreement here is significant. Neither will force Plato's words on this fundamental question in order to create a symmetry in metaphysic which the dialogues do not warrant. Whether he intended mind to be transcendent or not—at once "outside" and other than the Forms and "above" the ensouled οὐρανός—they dispute: but they agree that νοῦς and ψυχή are not

[1] W. F. R. Hardie, *A Study in Plato*, Oxford, 1936.

to be confused with and lost in the Form of the Good, still less in the other Forms.

But this quarrel has been from the beginning. We are only debating in modern terms the issue between Xenocrates and Crantor on the one side and Plutarch and Atticus on the other. Plutarch's *De Animae Procreatione in Timaeo*[1] and *Platonicae Quaestiones* survive to aid us, though other works of his have perished.[2] Mr Agar, in his little work on *Milton and Plato*, points out that Milton brought to the understanding of Plato a mind untrammelled either by the authoritative interpretations of the early middle ages or by the barbarous accretions of the renaissance. In the same way Plutarch and Atticus, in spite of their mistakes, may be said to put aside Xenocrates, Crantor, the Stoics and the Neopythagoreans and to approach Plato, more especially in the *Timaeus*, in a manner that promises to bring out the true sense of the original. However faulty Plutarch's attempt to take the history of the creation in the *Timaeus* literally and to bend the other dialogues into agreement with it, his interpretation, because of his insistence that Plato made ψυχή the αἰτία κινήσεως, is more valuable than the work of those who claim, rightly perhaps, that Plato was speaking of a historical creation διδασκαλίας χάριν but go on to misrepresent the διδασκαλία intended. For they ignore the necessity for Plato of an αἰτία κινήσεως other than the Form, and allow the ψυχή no metaphysical status unless it can be accommodated to the Forms and almost regarded as itself a Form. Likewise some modern mathematical physicists are prepared to recognise an unknowable ἐστώ τῶν πραγμάτων and something corresponding to "offprints of the Forms", but they will not recognise a distinct αἰτία κινήσεως or *causa gravitatis* as Burnet once expressed it.[3]

---

[1] Two interpretations of this tract have appeared recently: J. Helmer, *Zu Plutarch's De Animae Procreatione in Timaeo; ein Beitrag zum Verständnis des Platon-Deuters Plutarchs* (Mayr, Würzburg, 1937); P. Thévenaz, *L'Ame du Monde, le Devenir et la Matière chez Plutarque* (Paris, éd. les Belles Lettres, 1938).

[2] The *Catalogus* of Lamprias gives next to the *De Animae Procr.*: περὶ τοῦ γεγονέναι κατὰ Πλάτωνα τὸν κόσμον, and, as no. 66, πῶς ἡ ὕλη τῶν ἰδεῶν μετείληφεν ὅτι τὰ σώματα ποιεῖ;

[3] Burnet, *Greek Philosophy, Thales to Plato*, p. 335 n.

Both parties to the debate are wont to appeal to Aristotle; for, while he takes the *Timaeus* story literally, refusing the explanation of Xenocrates, he insists that Plato, like the Pythagoreans, never recognised the "efficient cause" or, alternatively, that he wrongly imagined that the Forms could be efficient as well as formal causes. One sentence only in the famous criticism of the Platonic doctrine of Forms, which appears twice in the *Metaphysics* as they have reached us,[1] seems to refer to the *Philebus* and the *Timaeus*. "What is this agency that 'works looking to the Forms'?" asks Aristotle.[2] It has naturally been argued that this shows that Aristotle did not regard the Αἰτία of the *Philebus* and the Δημιουργός of the *Timaeus* as integral parts of Plato's thought. But there is much to be taken into account before such a conclusion can be reached.

First of all, we have to remember that as soon as we turn from Aristotle's metaphysics to his physics, astronomy and psychology we find at once that the doctrines of the *Timaeus* and the *Philebus* are taken seriously, not least when they are rebutted. If we agree that these disciplines are precisely *not* metaphysics for Aristotle, it cannot be deduced that they, or rather the grounds and ultimate "causes" of them, were no part of Plato's metaphysic, or that Plato must have supposed the Forms to be ultimate in this realm because of Aristotle's doctrine of actualised forms. That is precisely the question that must not be begged. Moreover, the fact that for Aristotle κίνησις, and especially that κίνησις which is the being of the κυκλοφορικὸν σῶμα, never fits comfortably into the ὕλη—εἶδος scale is perhaps an indication that Aristotle never quite succeeded in expressing a doctrine which made the realised form the sole source of motion because he never abandoned Plato sufficiently to do so.[3]

Furthermore, Aristotle has imposed his own vocabulary and classification upon the subject-matter, and this must be allowed for

---

[1] Ar. *Metaph.* 990a 33 sqq., 1078b 7 sqq. (See J. M. Watson, *Aristotle's Criticisms of Plato*, Oxford, 1909.)

[2] Ar. *Metaph.* 991a 22, 1079b 27.

[3] Can the movement of the κυκλοφορικὸν σῶμα be called ἐνέργεια ἀτελής? The movement of the four bodies towards their form as they move towards their places might perhaps be so considered (*De Caelo* Δ 3, 310a 33 sqq.).

as much in Plato's case as in that of the pre-Socratics. We see at once that it is unreasonable to ask how many of Aristotle's four αἰτίαι were recognised by Heraclitus, but we are not so ready to see the unfairness of this question if asked concerning the Pythagoreans and Plato. The confusion is all the easier because Plato did use the word αἰτία, but with a different meaning. It keeps with him the sense of "personally responsible for" which appears in αἰτία ἑλομένου, ὁ δὲ θεὸς ἀναίτιος.[1] Perhaps in the *Phaedo* the αἰτίας ζήτησις on which Socrates embarked was a search for a reason and a plan rather than for a divine agency, in which Socrates already believed despite the Athenians' distrust of him. Yet even here such an antithesis is false, for it is a sustaining as well as a planning "cause" of coming-to-be and passing-away that is sought, and airs and waters and all such things could not be αἰτίαι in this sense.[2] For Plato as for Socrates there could not be a "material cause"—ὑποδοχή or τιθήνη γενέσεως is his expression, not αἰτία. The αἰτία there is the πλανωμένη αἰτία, which we shall find is a power of the psychic order.[3]

Even so, the refusal of Aristotle to allow that Plato recognised the efficient cause requires further explanation, for it was the one of Aristotle's four αἰτίαι which most nearly resembled what Plato meant by an αἰτία. We shall contend that Plato's αἰτία was intended seriously as a part of his metaphysic, to function as such an efficient cause. If this is so, how could Aristotle affect to ignore it so completely in his criticisms?[4]

First, perhaps, because his own doctrine of γένεσις was so definitely related to his biology. The opening of the *De Generatione Animalium* shows this, and the classification of *Metaphysics* A is hardly to be understood apart from its use there to define the efficient cause.[5]

---

[1] *Rep.* 617e.
[2] *Phaedo* 96a sqq., esp. ταύτῃ δὴ τῇ αἰτίᾳ ἥσθην, κ.τ.λ. *Ib.* 97c *init.* Cf. N. R. Murphy in *Class. Quart.* xxx, pp. 44–47.
[3] *V. infr.* ch. VI.
[4] Plato's notion of αἰτία differs radically from any modern notion of causality. On this see A. E. Taylor, *Commentary on Plato's Timaeus*, pp. 63–64 (note on *Tim.* 28a 4).
[5] Ar. *De Generatione Animalium* 715a 3–6.

Generation rather than technical production is the typical case of the informing of matter for Aristotle. Technical and artistic creation, the work of the Δημιουργός in the creation-story in the *Timaeus*, is for Aristotle to be understood by analogy with natural generation: the tool of the craftsman plays the part of the semen in generation in "carrying" the form to the matter.[1] Nothing is lacking to generation which is present in craftsmanship: craftsmanship imitates nature. With this view of the moving cause, we understand how Aristotle could speak so scathingly of Plato's poetic metaphors. Plato was less satisfactory even than the Pythagoreans, for while their number-form was in some sense immanent, Plato distinguished his doctrine from theirs by declaring the Forms to be separate. How, Aristotle asks, can anything come from these separated Forms in the accepted senses of "from"? Aristotle knows that "a man begets a man", but how can Plato's separated Forms control and initiate becoming?—γεννᾷ μὲν ἵππος, ἱππότης δὲ πῶς κυεῖ;

We ought to remember that Aristotle is not thinking of the *Timaeus* in making this criticism. The formulation of the doctrine of Forms which he is chiefly concerned to attack in these criticisms is that of the contemporary Academy, and since this ignored the αἰτία κινήσεως, it is not surprising that Aristotle made a complaint which Plutarch was also to make. Where Xenocrates is not aimed at, an early formulation like that of the *Phaedo* seems to be attacked: this also is particularly amenable to criticism. We shall try to show how Plato moved away from the account of ψυχή and κίνησις which we find in the third argument of the *Phaedo* tied up with the doctrine of Forms.[2] But Aristotle seems to leave out of account the reformulation presented by the *Sophistes*, and just as it would be wrong to infer that this reformulation was

---

[1] Ar. *De Generatione Animalium* 729 b 9 sqq., where Aristotle breaks off to "discuss the matter on general grounds", *ib.* 730 b 10, esp. b 20. "Nature uses the semen as a tool" (tr. Platt), but it remains true that this is a simile and that generation is the type to which the craftsman's act is analogous. Cf. *Phys.* B 8, 199a 16. I am indebted to articles by Mr M. B. Foster on "Christian Theology and Modern Science of Nature" in *Mind*, vols. XLIV, XLV. My cursory treatment of the matter does no justice to his interesting statement of the case, *ib.* XLIV, pp. 439–466.   [2] *V.* p. 7 *infr.*

no part of Plato's metaphysic from Aristotle's neglect of it, so one must not exclude on this ground the αἰτία which comes to the fore in the *Philebus* and in the *Timaeus*.

But after taking all these points into consideration, the *Timaeus* itself justifies to a very considerable degree Aristotle's impatience on the point chiefly at issue. The question how "offprints of the Forms enter and pass out from the realm of becoming" is left vague, even when the way to an explanation has been opened up by the threefold division of ὄν, χώρα and γένεσις.[1] We are told that it is τρόπος τις δύσφραστος and Aristotle has every right to protest against this evasion. Once in the classification of types of motion in the tenth book of the *Laws* we do seem to get some hint of what Plato believed about this question,[2] and it is clearly implied that behind the processes of γένεσις as behind all other bodily motions stands ψυχή, "the motion that has the power to move itself". Plutarch seems to have realised that there was a gap in Plato's teaching here, and to have hastened to fill it. One of his tracts according to the *Catalogus* of Lamprias was entitled πῶς ἡ ὕλη τῶν ἰδεῶν μετείληφεν ὅτι τὰ σώματα ποιεῖ; In the *De Animae Procreatione* he implies that we are to regard the world-soul of the chaos, "that which has its being in change and movement", as "set between that which makes and that which receives the offprints, distributing to the world of becoming the images received from the world of being".[3] Plutarch understands this, of course, of the literal creation of a cosmos in past history, but if we regard it as true constantly in history and if we remember that the Δημιουργός is better qualified to initiate the process than lesser ψυχαί, though they perhaps are directly responsible, we approach a positive doctrine which is con-

---

[1] *Tim.* 50c sqq.

[2] *Laws* x 894a *init.*; *infr.* pp. 105, 106.

[3] *De Animae Procr.* 1024c. Cf. J. Helmer, *op. cit.* p. 31: "Plutarch hat auf scharfsinnige Art diese Lücke im Gedankenbau Platons geschlossen. Warum mit einer Seele? Antwort: Die Abbildung geht unter Bewegung vor sich (*Tim.* 50c); wo Bewegung, da Seele; also ist die Urseele am Abbildungsvorgang beteiligt." Helmer explains διαδιδοῦσα in Plutarch "Sie verteilt hienieden die Bilder der Ideen ('verteilt' weil jede Idee durch viele Bilder dargestellt wird)".

sistent with the cosmology of the *Timaeus*. But it must be admitted
that this is a construction, and it ought to be far more explicit than
it is. But these considerations show that we must not idly ignore
Plato's words about the Demiurge, the Best Soul and the World
Soul, simply regarding them as "myth". The physics of the *Timaeus*
is μῦθος and can never be λόγος: it must aspire to be εἰκὼς μῦθος.[1]
But in the creation story and the account of the activities of the
Demiurge and the lesser souls we have μῦθος striving to become
λόγος—μῦθος, indeed, which is potentially λόγος because it concerns
ὄντως ὄντα. The protest in the *Sophistes*, an "ontological" dialogue,
against excluding "soul, mind, life, and reason" from the "perfectly
real" though they are other than the Forms leads to the conclusion
that Reality for Plato is more than the Forms. We have to study
this side of his thought, to examine its antecedents and to attempt
to show how it blends with the rest of his teaching.

[1] On this *v*. ch. v *infr.*

CHAPTER I

PLATO'S LATER PHILOSOPHY OF MOTION

To speak of Plato's "later" philosophy of motion is not to imply that he held an "earlier" doctrine and modified it in the cosmology of the *Timaeus* and in the natural theology of the *Laws.* The dialogues do not present us with a coherent metaphysical system, but they do show at least as much consistency in the treatment of κίνησις as in the treatment of εἴδη. But the doctrine of κίνησις may be called a "later" doctrine because all the important passages (save two that call for special consideration, one from the *Cratylus*, the other from the *Phaedrus*) belong to the later group of critical dialogues which begins with the *Theaetetus*. This doctrine, therefore, may be regarded as a development of Plato's thinking in the years of the established Academy, when the disaster to his Sicilian expedition had driven him to look deeper than did the astronomers and mathematicians who worked with him into the source of those regular, law-abiding motions which they were making the subject of detailed study and constant discussion. Nor will this development in Plato's thought surprise us when we remember his appeal at the end of the ninth book of the *Republic* from the mounting ἀνομία of men and states on earth to the perfect εὐνομία of the οὐρανός.[1]

(a) The Cratylus

Plato's early following of Cratylus and his "familiarity with the Heraclitean opinions", which is attested by Aristotle in the *Meta-*

---

[1] *Rep.* 592b. Adam *ad loc.* questions Steinhart's contention that *Tim.* 47b sqq., 90d sqq. are directly related to this passage. οὐρανός has Christian connotations for most of us which distort our judgment of this passage: in our acceptance or rejection of these we are in equal danger of ignoring the established Pythagorean meaning of the word and the deeply religious tone pervading the whole passage and not confined to the word. The εὐνομία of the οὐρανός is, for the Pythagorean, its ὁμοίωσις θεῷ κατὰ τὸ δυνατόν. For Plato to turn, as he does, to the παράδειγμα ἐν οὐρανῷ is in line with this tradition and marks the beginning of his later glorification of astronomy.

physics, square so exactly with what we find in Plato's *Cratylus* that it is difficult to imagine how its closing section can be regarded as anything but autobiographical on Plato's part and of first importance for an understanding of the development of his thought. It is unfortunate, therefore, that Professor Taylor seems to have felt compelled to minimise its importance in his strict loyalty to his own and the late Professor Burnet's position on the question of the "historical Socrates".[1] But it is perhaps more significant still to study the reasons which led Max Warburg recently to deny that the Cratylus of the dialogue represents the Heraclitean at all and to identify him with Heraclides Ponticus.[2] One of his reasons alone concerns us here. He maintains that κίνησις in the *Cratylus* represents not external processes of change but "that motion the source of which, for a Greek thinker, must be the soul".[3] Perhaps the passage offering strongest support to this contention is the "etymology" of δίκαιον at *Cratylus* 411 a–413 d. This passage brings out what is common to all philosophers of the Ionian tradition. We need not

[1] A. E. Taylor, *Plato, the Man and his Work*, p. 76. Plato's connections with Cratylus are not denied, but their importance is minimised and the whole dialogue is related back to the *Euthydemus* rather than forward to the later critical group. There is very little English work on the *Cratylus*—virtually none since Jackson's dissertation in the Cambridge Praelections of 1906. Haag's recent work contains a *Literaturverzeichnis* in which no English name appears, and Haag is not to blame for this.

[2] Max Warburg, *Zwei Fragen zum Kratylos* (Neue philologische Untersuchungen herausg. von W. Jaeger, Vtes Heft, 1929). Warburg's contention was based on his acceptance of Reinhardt's dictum that Plato knew Heraclitus only through the Heracliteans and on Cohn's earlier thesis (*De Heraclide Pontico etymologiarum scriptore antiquissimo*, Breslau 1884). He was refuted at length by Dahlmann in a review in the *Deutsche Literaturzeitung*, 1929. Warburg's second *Frage* is the place of the dialogue in the *Reihenfolge*; he seeks to show that it is "critical" and comes immediately before the *Theaetetus*.

[3] "Denn das πάντα ῥεῖ des Dialoges entspringt gar nicht mehr der relativen Skepsis der Sophistenzeit, sondern κίνησις wird hier offenbar als positiv schöpferischer Vorgang empfunden. Das zeigt sich schon darin, dass zur Bezeugung der heraklitischen Wahrheit die Urgötter der Theogonien, also kosmogonische Prinzipien angeführt werden. Es handelt sich hier nicht mehr um κίνησις als μεταβολή sondern eher um jene κίνησις deren Prinzip für griechische Anschauung die ψυχή ist." Warburg, *op. cit.* p. 11.

agree with Warburg that Cratylus cannot appropriately achieve this appreciation, or, if we do allow this, we must not suppose Plato himself incapable of achieving it at the time he wrote the *Cratylus*. We must therefore assert that one element in Plato's later doctrine of motion was present from the beginning—an appreciation of the significance of the Ionian conception of the ἀρχή. But it was only after this had been related to the Orphic-Pythagorean ideas of the soul and all these ideas had been reconciled with the doctrine of the Forms that the full valuation of κίνησις within the Platonic scheme of things became possible.

(b) The Phaedrus

The relating in Plato's thought of the Ionian ἀρχή to the Orphic-Pythagorean immortal ψυχή is revealed in a passage which arises abruptly in the second discourse of Socrates in the *Phaedrus*, and in its style differs markedly alike from the myth that follows it and from the rest of the dialogue. To show that the lover's madness is a gift from heaven, Socrates says, we must examine the nature of the soul, its actions and passions. Its nature is to be immortal, and this is the proof of it:

Soul is immortal in all its forms.[1] For that which is ever in motion is immortal,[2] while that which imparts to something else the motion

---

[1] *Phaedrus* 245 c 5 sqq. At 246 b *infr.* we find the sentence πᾶσα ἡ ψυχή παντὸς ἐπιμελεῖται τοῦ ἀψύχου, on which Schleiermacher's note is: "Alles Geistige wird hier als Eins betrachtet ohne Unterschied des Ranges und der Persönlichkeit" (*Platons Werke*[2], I, p. 382). Even if we do translate ψυχὴ πᾶσα here by "every soul" it cannot be said that the argument proves anything concerning the individual soul: πᾶν σῶμα at 245 e 4 *infr.* seems the counterpart of ψυχὴ πᾶσα here and both seem to have a meaning approximating to πᾶσα ἡ ψυχή and πᾶν τὸ ἄψυχον at 246 b.

[2] M. Robin in his recent edition in the Budé series prints αὐτοκίνητον on the evidence, it seems, of Oxyrhynchus Pap. 1016. But, apart from the hardihood of this, the argument is vitiated by this reading. It is true that we have here an axiom, but this is in the major premiss, τὸ ἀεικίνητον ἀθάνατον. The sentence τὸ δ' ἄλλο... ζωῆς establishes that *only* τὸ αὐτο-κίνητον is ἀεικίνητον and this would be otiose in Robin's version. Alcmaeon had held that τὸ ἀεικίνητον ἀθάνατον (Ar. *De Anima* A 2, 405 a 29; cf. Krische, *Forschungen*, I, p. 76) and Plato could presume that he had good grounds for treating this as axiomatic.

it receives from elsewhere, being liable to cease to move is therefore liable to cease to live. Thus it is only the self-moving which, being constant to its own nature, never ceases to be in motion and which, moreover, is the fount and origin[1] of everything else that moves. Now an origin is ungenerated. For all that comes into being must of necessity come into being from an origin but the origin itself cannot come into being from anything. For if the origin came into being from something else, the coming into being would not arise from it as origin.[2] Further, since it is ungenerated it must also be indestructible. For once an origin is destroyed it can never come into being from anything else nor can anything else come into being from it—if we allow that everything must come into being from an origin. It follows, then, that the self-moving is the origin of motion; and it can no more be destroyed than it can come into being, else the whole heaven and all that is coming-into-being within it must collapse and come to a standstill and never thereafter possess anything that can cause them to move and bring them into being. Since, then, the self-moving has been proved to be immortal, one may now safely say that precisely this is the essence and definition[3] of the soul. For body everywhere, when receiving its motion from outside, is without soul, but when receiving its motion from within itself is ensouled; for this is the characteristic nature of soul. If it is really so, then, that the self-moving is soul and nothing else, it must follow necessarily that soul is ungenerated and immortal.

[1] I have tried by the use of the word "origin" to suggest something like Anaximander's ἄπειρον treated as ἀρχή, as it is by Aristotle (*Phys.* Γ 3, 203 b 3 sqq.: see Cornford's note in the Loeb ed.), but not necessarily the wider connotations of ἀρχή in Aristotle which tend to be in our mind in reading this passage.

[2] Burnet accepted Buttmann's ἔτι ἀρχή following Iamblichus, Timaeus Locrus (in Theodoretus), and Cicero's translation of the passage (*Tusc. Disp.* I 23). But there is no parallel for ἔτι γένοιτο meaning ἔτι εἴη, and this is intolerable in a sentence in which γίγνεσθαι has been thrice used in a technical sense. We must therefore accept the *lectio difficilior* of the MSS. and find an interpretation other than the nonsensical one that if an ἀρχή comes into being from something prior, what it comes from is not an ἀρχή. I have therefore understood the phrase as meaning that if B is regarded as the ἀρχή of a γένεσις C, then, if B is not an ἀρχή but itself has a more ultimate ἀρχή, A, the γένεσις at C no longer proceeds directly from B as ἀρχή but from A through B.

[3] οὐσία καὶ λόγος here anticipate the longer treatment at *Laws* x 895 c sqq. (*v.* Ritter, *Commentar, ad loc.*): for a discussion of the elaboration of this classification at *Ep.* vii 342 b sqq. see Howald, *Briefe*, p. 35; W. Andreae, *Philologus*, LXXXVIII (1922); A. E. Taylor, *Mind*, vol. xxi (1912).

We may begin our discussion of this passage by recalling a brilliant excursion into this field by J. B. Bury in an article in the *Journal of Philology* for 1886. There Bury combats the view[1] that the *Phaedrus* is an early dialogue chiefly on the ground that the argument for the immortality of the soul in this dialogue presupposes and advances upon the arguments in the *Phaedo*. "The category of αὐτοκινησία (τὸ αὐτὸ κινοῦν) is the solution Plato has discovered for the difficulty which exercised him as to aitiology when he was studying Anaxagoras."[2] We need to see the wider context of the argument, its pre-Socratic antecedents and its relation to the *Timaeus* and the *Laws*, but the fact remains that Bury has indicated for us the precise step in the development of Plato's thinking which it represents.

Several scholars have pointed out the antecedents of this passage in pre-Socratic thought. Krische[3] noted the connection with Alcmaeon's saying that the soul is immortal because it is ever in motion like the sun, moon and stars. Susemihl, in his work *Die genetische Entwicklung der platonischen Philosophie*,[4] treating of the argument as a whole suggests that the force of the ἀπόδειξις consists in the use of the Parmenidean arguments concerning τὸ ὄν to establish the reality and indestructibility of the ἀρχή.[5] We may well agree

---

[1] A view which even Jackson (*Cambridge Praelections* (i)) could defend as late as 1906.

[2] J. B. Bury, "Some Questions connected with Plato's *Phaidros*", *Journal of Philology*, xv, p. 84.

[3] *Die theologischen Lehren der griechischen Denker, Forschungen*, I, pp. 76 sqq. (Göttingen, 1840).

[4] Leipzig, 1855.

[5] *Op. cit.* I, p. 229. Susemihl also points out the parallel between the sun chariot of Parmenides and the *Phaedrus* myth. This parallel offers us a better interpretation of the procession of souls under the leadership of the gods (which we find in a closely similar form at *Timaeus* 41 e *init.*) than attempts to explain the *Phaedrus* by reference to the Pythagorean central-fire cosmogony. M. Robin's note on *Phaedrus* 247 a *init.* in the Budé edition shows the difficulty of fitting any astronomical scheme to the details of the myth: the expedients required keep the Pythagoreans with their ἀντίχθων well in countenance. Professor Taylor has suggested that the details of this passage (and also perhaps of the closing sentence of the *Critias*) are sufficiently accounted for by the common altar at Athens of the δώδεκα θεοί.

that the reasoning is intended to be metaphysical—in Plato's language, that it concerns an ἀρχή which is to be regarded as ὄντως ὄν. Perhaps this is not stated explicitly till we come to the *Sophistes* passage that we have to consider later, but we ought to remember when we come to read the *Sophistes* passage that ψυχή is not a vague term: its nature and functions have been defined here with far greater precision than Plato was wont to allow himself. Nevertheless we cannot admit Susemihl's contention that the passage is Parmenidean if by that he means that it anticipates in the same way as Parmenides did the reasoning found later in the "ontological argument" in Christian theology. Have we not rather in this argument an anticipation of the "cosmological argument" of which Aristotle has generally been considered the father? We are told that if the ἀρχή were destructible, all the γένεσις arising from it would collapse and fail.[1] But this is precisely Aristotle's argument from the existence of motion, and in particular of the constant rotation of the πρῶτος οὐρανός, to the existence of the Unmoved Mover and the eternity of the world. Indeed it was this passage which Plutarch had to explain away in order to vindicate Plato's consistency and his own literal interpretation of the creation story of the *Timaeus*;[2] for it had been a proof-text for the Platonists and Stoics desiring to subscribe to the Aristotelian doctrine of the eternity of the world and it was to become matter of debate in the Christian arguments concerning the doctrine of creation.

The passage seems to imply a close union of ψυχή and σῶμα which meets in advance some of Aristotle's criticism of the self-moved as the prime mover. In spite of what seems a sheer dichotomy between that which can move itself and that which receives and transmits motion, it is clear that Plato thinks of the two as conjoined in reality and implying one another. πᾶσα ἡ ψυχὴ παντὸς ἐπιμελεῖται τοῦ ἀψύχου is the full conclusion of the argument—it is

---

[1] This reappears at *Theaetetus* 153d (a passage which throws light on Aristotle's view of the work of the Sun in the λοξὸς κύκλος in *de Gen. et Corr.* B) and at *Laws* x 895a sqq.: εἰ σταίη πως τὰ πάντα κ.τ.λ.

[2] οὐδὲ γὰρ σοφιστῇ κραιπαλῶντι, πόθεν γε δὴ Πλάτωνι, τοιαύτην ἄν τις ἀναθείη, περὶ οὓς ἐσπουδάκει μάλιστα τῶν λόγων, ταραχὴν καὶ ἀνωμαλίαν. κ.τ.λ.: *de animae procr.* 1016a–c.

not merely a demonstration of the indestructibility of soul. Unfortunately Plato never explains how this ἐπιμέλεια functions—as we shall see, he is lamentably vague in treating of psychophysical questions—but it remains true that a "cosmological argument" which used the reasoning of the *Phaedrus* rather than of Aristotle's *Physics* would seek to show not only the existence of a first mover but a constant sustaining and providential activity of which the ordered universe is the direct manifestation.

But we are concerned at the moment with the more immediate significance of the passage in the development of Plato's thought, and to estimate this we must turn, as Bury did, to compare this passage with the "third proof" of the *Phaedo*, the proof of the immortality of the soul based on the doctrine of Forms.[1] This bases itself on two postulates: "opposite Forms exclude each other", and "a particular of which a given Form is essentially predicated excludes the opposite of that Form". Thus snow, which is not Coldness, excludes Heat, and fire, which is not Heat, excludes Coldness. Similarly soul, which is not Life, excludes Death. The weaknesses of this proof need hardly be exposed: Socrates is made to encourage Simmias's hesitation at the end of it and Plato seems to be insisting that the argument is ambivalent and that the only unquenchable evidence for immortality is Socrates himself, who has the faith and courage to say "Bury me if you can catch me". Yet the weak points of the proof do provide us with an indication that at the time of writing the *Phaedo* Plato was feeling after a doctrine of ψυχή that would give it its true place in the scheme of things and give some metaphysical ground for the Orphic belief in the imperishable individual soul. Two points in the argument stand out in this connection. When Coldness encroaches on fire, the fire is either destroyed or retires,[2] and similarly when Death encroaches on the soul either alternative should be possible; but, says Plato, that which does

[1] *Phaedo* 102a–107b. Taylor, *op. cit.* pp. 204–206. I have accepted Taylor's phrase "essential predication" as a shorthand expression, but the argument is ontological, not logical, and any full account of it would have to deal with "encroachment", "withdrawal", "destruction", as well as "possession" and "carrying"—none of them logical expressions.

[2] 103d *fin.*

not "admit" death is ἀθάνατον and this is inherently ἀνώλεθρον: therefore the possibility of destruction does not arise in the case of the soul and it retires unharmed at death. This blatant *petitio principii* rests on the axiom that τὸ ἀθάνατον· is ἀνώλεθρον. This could be regarded as axiomatic alike by one who held the Orphic faith and by one who believed in a divine φύσις like the ever-living fire of Heraclitus. Thus Plato really calls into service, to gain his point in the *Phaedo*, that very alliance between the physicists' imperishable ground of the universe and the Orphic faith in the imperishable soul which appears in our *Phaedrus* passage fully worked out, and explained, as Bury says, by the common category of τὸ αὐτὸ αὐτὸ κινοῦν. Thus a weak point in the *Phaedo* proof, a blatant *petitio principii* in fact, points to Plato's real line of development in his thinking about the soul. In the second place, there is the very evident difficulty of positing a "Form of Life", as distinct from the Form of Living Creature which we find later in the αὐτόζωον of the *Timaeus*. This "Form of Life" is essentially predicated of ψυχή, but might, presumably, be essentially predicated of other things: in more Platonic terms, other things than souls might "carry with them"[1] the Form of Life. This difficulty is surmounted in the *Phaedrus* argument where soul and life are regarded as co-extensive and identified with the self-moving, but we ask ourselves how the difficulty in the *Phaedo* arose in the first place. One reason, no doubt, would be that Life rather than Soul is the opposite of Death, but the more subtle difficulty seems to be to conceive of a "Form of Soul" at all: by means of the class of "things of which given Forms are essentially predicated" this difficulty is evaded, but the evasion is manifest. Why, then, should Plato find it possible to conceive Forms of Life and of Death but not a Form of Soul? A full answer to this question would involve a thorough discussion of the passage in which Socrates is made to describe his turning to the σκέψις ἐν λόγοις as a δεύτερος πλοῦς, but this would take us too far afield.[2] We need

[1] ἐπιφέρειν, *Phaedo* 105 d.
[2] Bury's statement that in "the category of αὐτοκινησία" Plato found the solution of the difficulties he had felt concerning the αἰτία in reading Anaxagoras is, no doubt, too simple a solution and one which solves

only remark that if the Forms are after all not the "directest" way of dealing with γένεσις καὶ φθορά still less can they help Plato in giving a metaphysical account of ψυχή. The earlier part of the *Phaedo* leaves us with a soul that separates herself from body so as to cognise the eternally real,[1] but she is not herself regarded as one of these eternal Forms, still less as one of the passing embodiments of one of these Forms in the flux of becoming. Yet the whole argument falls if soul is not as much an existent as the Forms are. Simmias is made to approve the conclusion that there is "equal necessity"[2] for the existence of Forms and the pre-existence (which involves the eternal persistence) of the soul. This is the position which Socrates may well have held, but which Plato certainly approved as his later dialogues tell us.[3] He seems to have made one attempt, the third proof of the *Phaedo*,[4] to fit the soul into the scheme of eternal Forms by postulating a Form of Life. This attempt manifestly failed and therefore the metaphysical problem of that which is ὄντως ὄν but not a Form remained with Plato until it found final solution in the *Sophistes*. The tenth book of the *Republic* and the *Phaedrus* passage before us show us two attempts to clarify and define the metaphysical status of the ψυχή without attempting to

the problem of the historical Socrates with a shocking complacency. Yet it supplies us with a very useful clue. The closing sentences of Mr Murphy's recent article in the *Classical Quarterly* (XXX, pp. 40–47) would seem to point us in a similar direction.

[1] See especially *Phaedo* 79 d.

[2] καὶ ἴση ἀνάγκη ταὐτά τε εἶναι (sc. ἃ θρυλοῦμεν ἀεί) καὶ τὰς ἡμετέρας ψυχὰς πρὶν καὶ ἡμᾶς γεγονέναι, καὶ εἰ μὴ ταῦτα, οὐδὲ τάδε, *Phaedo* 76 e.

[3] On the question of "the historical Socrates" I try to state a position acceptable to all save those who press *Ep.* II 314c so strongly as to hold that Plato's philosophy is confined to the ἄγραφα δόγματα.

[4] It may be the case that Plato is deliberately confining himself in this proof to arguments that were actually used by Pythagoreans who were "friends of the Forms" and also friends of Socrates. There would be dramatic propriety in representing Socrates as employing their terms and then declaring that the original hypotheses must be stringently tested. But whether Plato is artfully revealing the incompetency of the Forms doctrine thus stated to deal with γένεσις καὶ φθορά and with the ψυχή or whether he can be seen here working the matter out for himself, the conclusion is the same.

relate it to the Forms doctrine. The *Republic*[1] with its doctrine that soul alone is not destroyed by its σύμφυτον κακόν (a point in apparent contradiction to the final proof of the *Phaedo*) is really concerned to vindicate the Orphic belief in the simple imperishable soul which might seem to have been endangered by a Pythagorean tripartition in the main part of the dialogue. We return to the thought of the soul as "akin to" the eternal which was the essence of the teaching of Socrates in the *Phaedo*.[2] The *Phaedrus* passage takes this up and unites it with what had been in Plato's mind from the first associations with Cratylus—the realisation that the Ionian doctrine of the ἀρχή was not to be identified with the flux-metaphysic of the Heracliteans but proclaimed a *Weltgrund* of a "psychic" order as the ultimate reality. These two elements then, the Orphic ψυχή and the Ionian φύσις, unite in the term τὸ αὐτὸ κινοῦν and thus the *Phaedrus* passage takes its place as Plato's first constructive attempt to deal with κίνησις as an element in the universe.

(c) The Theaetetus

The *Theaetetus* might be supposed to be of primary importance for a study of Plato's doctrines of motion because of the elaborate reduction of perceiver, percept and perception to a complex of motions in the doctrine of οἱ κομψότεροι,[3] which is generally agreed to represent Plato's own elaboration of contemporary Heraclitean ideas. But this, after all, is only an elaboration, and the contribution of the dialogue to the doctrine of motion is almost as negative as its contribution to the doctrine of Forms. This is due, no doubt, to the very fact that the εἴδη are in abeyance and no further step can be taken in the development of the doctrine of κίνησις until this has been reconciled with the εἴδη. We do find, of course, interesting descriptions of the Heraclitean school and a recognition of the "antiquity" of the flux-metaphysic: these points will concern us

[1] *Rep.* x 608d–612a.
[2] Comparing *Rep.* x 611e with *Phaedo* 79d the only advance we can trace in the former is perhaps a clearer statement that the soul in itself, and not simply quâ knower, shares the eternity of the Forms.
[3] *Theaet.* 156a.

later on.[1] The field is arrayed for the γιγαντομαχία of the *Sophistes*,[2] but this cannot begin because of Plato's refusal to examine Parmenides and the Eleatics in a dialogue from which the Forms are excluded. He does, however, before leaving the Heracliteans, give us a summary of the kinds of physical motion which seems to be of more than passing importance. Earlier in the dialogue he had offered, as part of the doctrine of οἱ κομψότεροι, a division of motion into "two species of infinite extent, one manifesting the active factor (in αἴσθησις) the other the passive";[3] but this division does not help us in any wider field than that of sheer αἴσθησις, and is hardly exhaustive even there, for Plato admits τό τέ τινι συνελθὸν καὶ ποιοῦν ἄλλῳ αὖ προσπεσὸν πάσχον ἀνεφάνη.[4] But the division we reach at 181 b is evidently intended to have real validity. It arises out of a conversation between Socrates and Theodorus.[5]

Socrates. Well then, if you are as concerned as this, we had better examine the question. It seems to me that any examination of the nature of motion should begin from an enquiry into what is meant by saying of "all things" that they are "in motion". What I am trying to say is this. Do these men recognise but one species of motion, or am I right in supposing that they recognise two? I trust I shall not be left to hold the opinion by myself: come in with me and face the risks of holding it by my side. Tell me, do you apply the term "motion" to the exchange by a given object of one position for another and equally to its rotation in one fixed position?
Theodorus. Yes, I do.
Socrates. Let this be one species of motion, then. Now suppose a thing stays in the same place and does not revolve, but that it grows old or turns black instead of white or hard instead of soft or undergoes some other kind of alteration. Does not this merit description as a second species of motion?
Theodorus. It must.
Socrates. So I posit these two species of motion—alteration and locomotion.
Theodorus. These are the two species.

We have here the first formal recognition of the rotation of the sphere on its own axis about a fixed centre as a "kind" of motion,

[1] In ch. II.   [2] *Theaet.* 179d–184a.   [3] *Ib.* 156a.
[4] *Ib.* 157a.   [5] *Ib.* 181b *fin.* sqq.

and this will be of cardinal importance for the fusion of astronomy, psychology and metaphysics that will meet us in the *Timaeus*. The point has in fact been made earlier, in the course of the discussion of the maxim of Contradiction in the fourth book of the *Republic*,[1] concerning spinning-tops, but now we find this rotation recognised as one of the great classes of motion—the motion, as will later appear, that is perfectly combined with rest and alone fitted to be the εἰκών of the motions of νοῦς.

The introduction of ἀλλοίωσις here probably has an immediate relevance to the ποιότητες of the subsequent argument, and these are probably no more permanent elements in Plato's thought than are the κοινά of 185 b. But in its wider bearing ἀλλοίωσις here covers all the kinds of motion which are exhibited in the interfusion of the four bodies and in the processes of growth and decay as we shall find them in the *Timaeus*. Here, however, there is no hint that all these alterations are reducible ultimately to forms of locomotion: for that we have to look even beyond the *Parmenides*, to the full classification of *Laws* x.

It is important to remember that this passage does no more than classify external bodily motions—there is no hint of "the motion that moves itself"—the tenth "kind" of the *Laws* classification. Heidel[2] and Lutoslawski[3] by ignoring this limitation read far-reaching significance into the passage which it will hardly bear. Plato is doing little more here than sketching out the classes of motions he will later analyse in detail: he is not saying anything at all concerning the cause of motion, the αἰτία κινήσεως in Plato's sense of the word αἰτία.

(d) The Parmenides

We have said that the γιγαντομαχία of the *Sophistes* was impossible in the *Theaetetus* because Plato could not examine Parmenides and the Eleatics in a dialogue from which the Forms had been deliberately excluded. The logical order of development, there-

---

[1] *Rep.* 436b sqq.
[2] "Qualitative Change in pre-Socratic Philosophy", art. in *Archiv für Geschichte der Philosophie*, Band XIX.
[3] *Origin and Growth of Plato's Logic*, pp. 365 sqq.

fore, requires us to consider the *Parmenides* next, whether it is
historically prior to the *Theaetetus* or not. Here we have the
technique of wrestling with Father Parmenides, or rather with his
younger followers, developed to a nicety. As a result, it is easy to
show in the *Sophistes* that reality as such does not necessarily imply
absence of motion and that κίνησις καὶ ʒωὴ καὶ ψυχὴ καὶ φρόνησις
may be and are elements in "the whole of True Being".

We are chiefly concerned in the *Parmenides* with the second
hypothesis and especially with the added section on becoming in
time (beginning at 155 e). Twice elsewhere, at 138 b in the first hypothesis and at 162 d in the sixth, we find φορά and ἀλλοίωσις, the two
forms of physical motion distinguished in the *Theaetetus*. They
cannot belong to the One simply or to a non-existent Being. But
both of these sections are parallel in scope to the addendum to
Hypothesis II, save that they are negative while it is positive. Therefore Plato uses in them a short description of the kinds of motion
which he elaborates in the positive passage.

The passage can only be understood in the light of the general
interpretation of the first and second hypotheses. The interpretation
followed here is intended to be in keeping with Professor Cornford's
recent book,[1] but it might very well hold good on other estimates
of the purpose of the dialogue. The Eleatics must be given a stronger
dose of their own physic. The consequences of affirming One Being
must be rigorously examined. If the One, simple and absolute, be
affirmed, it cannot have limits or shape or be in space, or be whole,
like itself, exist, or be knowable (and Parmenides had insisted on all
these σήματα) any more than it can become, grow, change or have
parts or internal difference (which Parmenides had denied). On the
other hand, once posit One *Being* and you must deduce indefinite
plurality, extension, shape, sameness and difference, rest and motion.
This is the second hypothesis of the second part of the dialogue.
The answer to the question "What realm of being is Plato describing here?" would be in the first instance "That which is
logically deducible from the Eleatic affirmation of One Being,
especially in view of Parmenides's description of it as a well-rounded
sphere". Once grant even "being", let alone extension and shape,

[1] *Plato and Parmenides* (Kegan Paul, 1939).

to the One, and you must also posit plurality, parts, likeness and unlikeness, rest and motion. Thus when Parmenides asserts a sphere full of being he has no right to deny to it motion and change. Therefore in the sense in which the sphere "exists", motion also "exists": the "sign" ἀκίνητον is arbitrary.

We need not enter into the controversy as to the nature of the Being described in the second hypothesis. No doubt the hypothesis is something more than an *argumentum ad hominem*: it does imply something positive in Plato's own view of the universe. It is perhaps significant that here, as in the case of the μεικτόν of the *Philebus*, an attempt has been made to assert a reference to the Forms exclusively.[1] The fact that increase and motion are recognised characters of the Being described makes any such reference very difficult. What we seem to have here is a recognition of the "being", in a sense, of natural physical objects, and, if so, the third class of the *Philebus* is prepared for by the reasoning of the *Parmenides*.

We are concerned, however, with the description of the kinds of motion. Plato holds that certain kinds of motion are logically deducible from the hypothesis of One Being. These are coming into being and passing away, combination and separation, likeness and unlikeness, increase and diminution. The parallel to Aristotle's classification in the *Physics* strikes us immediately. Plato himself was to enter upon a still more subtle classification in *Laws* x, based on the physical account of the interfusion of the four bodies in the *Timaeus*. But this passage helps us to explain how a degree of "being" can be attributed to that which becomes. This has often proved puzzling to interpreters of the *Philebus* and the *Laws* and has forced them to drag in the Forms to provide an unsatisfying explanation. ἔστιν δὲ ὄντως ὄν, ὁπόταν μένῃ at *Laws* 894a can only be understood of the degree of "being" asserted in this hypothesis.

Therefore the *Parmenides* gives us a logical classification of the kinds of physical motions which in a sense "exist" in the realm of

---

[1] See R. G. Bury, *The Philebus of Plato*, Intro. p. lxiv, for a summary of the views of Jackson and others. Diès so interprets the *Parmenides* "hypothesis" in the Budé edition of the dialogue (see Cornford, *Plato and Parmenides*, pp. 193, 194).

γεγενημένη οὐσία as it was later to be described in the *Philebus*.[1] Strictly all we have is a deduction of logical consequences from a hypothesis, but the *Parmenides* and the *Philebus* passages must be read together. This, however, does not tell us anything about the αἰτία, which is the fourth factor in πάντα τὰ νῦν ὄντα ἐν τῷ παντί as this is divided into factors in the *Philebus*. This αἰτία in its relation to ψυχή and νοῦς is none the less a real and necessary element in the scheme of things, and we shall find in the *Sophistes* how a place equal in honour with the static Forms is at last secured for it.

(e) The Sophistes

We must turn, then, to the *Sophistes*, where the violence proved necessary is done to Father Parmenides and the dialectical philosopher is distinguished from the eristic Sophist and allotted his true province. The passage we have chiefly to consider begins at 242b and goes on to 251a. Part of it is often described as the γιγαντομαχία, but it is really a discussion of the meaning and extent of τὸ παντελῶς ὄν which is necessary before the definition of the dialectician can be reached. Most of the earlier philosophers are hinted at, and their conception of the nature of things is considered and classified. The passage contains three sections, of which the last two overlap. In each section we find an antithesis, and philosophers are grouped according to their affirmation of the opposing positions. According to the terms of each antithesis, however, the alignment of actual philosophers would vary. In each case Plato criticises the extreme positions and proposes a synthesis. In the case of the second antithesis, however (that between materialists in general and idealists in general), the synthesis proposed loses itself in the setting forth and the discussion of the third antithesis between the belief in a moving or a motionless reality. These antitheses may be briefly stated:

(*a*) 242b-245e. The conflict of pluralists with monists.[2]
(*b*) 245e-249d. The conflict of materialists with idealists (the "friends of the Forms"). This is the γιγαντομαχία proper.

---

[1] *V.* pp. 28, 29 *infr.*
[2] In the first section (pluralists *v.* monists) it might seem that only the

(c) 248a–251a. The conflict between believers in universal motion and believers in a motionless reality.[1]

It is only the third of these antitheses that really concerns us. It leads up to the conclusion at 250c that the real is neither in motion nor at rest κατὰ τὴν αὐτοῦ φύσιν and part of it calls for closer examination.[2] The Eleatic Stranger is speaking with Theaetetus.

Stranger. I see your point.[3] You mean this. If knowing is to be regarded as a kind of acting, it follows necessarily that being known becomes in its turn a kind of being acted upon. Now Reality according to this argument is acted upon in so far as it is known, and in so far therefore it is moved—which is a thing that could not happen to the motionless reality we described.

Theaetetus. Exactly.

Stranger. But tell me, in Heaven's name: are we really to be so easily convinced that in actual fact the Whole of True Being has in Itself neither motion nor life nor Soul nor intelligence—that it neither lives nor thinks, but is an Awful, Holy, Unmoved and forever Established Thing—without any mind in it?[4]

---

latter (i.e. Parmenides) is really criticised; but criticism of the pluralists is clearly implied at the beginning—μῦθον δοκεῖ μοι ἕκαστος διηγεῖσθαι κ.τ.λ.

[1] The difficulty of discriminating (b) and (c) is aggravated in two ways:

(i) The "Gods" are described as breaking up the so-called reality of the materialist "Giants" into γένεσις φερομένη (246b). This recalls the tactics of the *Theaetetus* and it has been assumed that the battle rages on the issue of motion and motionlessness from the beginning. But it does not. It rages on the wider issue of "materialism" and "idealism".

(ii) 248a–249d is at once the statement of the compromise desired on the issue of (b) from the idealists (to meet the concession of the materialists that they will regard δύναμις as a ὅρος of the real) and the setting out of the issue of (c). Hence arises, it would seem, the difficulty raised by Cornford at 248d (*Plato's Theory of Knowledge*, p. 240 n. 3) that the argument that, in the act of being known, τὸ ὂν πάσχει, is not taken up in the conclusion. This argument is necessary to the symmetry of (b) but irrelevant to (c).

[2] *Sophistes* 248d fin. sqq.

[3] Heindorf's distribution of the dialogue seems required. I treat τόδε γε as taking up Theaetetus's answer immediately before and not referring further back to the "idealists" as Cornford would seem to take it in translating "*Their* point is...".

[4] νοῦν οὐκ ἔχον. "With no sense in it" is perhaps the right rendering. If so, this is a wicked addition no devout Eleatic could allow himself.

Theaetetus. Well, I must grant you, my friend, that this is a strange doctrine, if we are asked to assent to it.

Stranger. But are we to say that it has mind and yet has no life?

Theaetetus. Impossible.

Stranger. But if we say it has them both, can we deny that it has them resident in a soul?

Theaetetus. How else could it have them?

Stranger. But then, if it is admittedly possessed of life, mind and soul can we imagine its being, for all its vitality, completely static and immune from motion?[1]

Theaetetus. All this seems quite unreasonable to me.

Stranger. Then that which is moved and motion itself are to be admitted real.

Theaetetus. Yes.

Stranger. We conclude, then, Theaetetus, first, that if real things are motionless,[2] there can be no mind anywhere to exercise itself on any object.

Theaetetus. Exactly.

Stranger. But, secondly, if we admit that all things pass and are moved, by this doctrine too we shall remove this same factor of mind from the totality of the real.

Theaetetus. How so?

Stranger. Do you think that, if there were no freedom from motion, there could be anything that abides constant in the same condition and in the same respects?

Theaetetus. There could not.

Stranger. And can you make out mind as existing anywhere without such abiding objects?

Theaetetus. Certainly not.

Stranger. Well then with all the forces of reason we must meet the enemy who makes dogmatic assertion on any question while at the same time cutting away the very basis of knowledge, intelligence and mind?

Theaetetus. Most certainly.

Stranger. So it appears that the mind of the philosopher—the true philosopher who places these as valuable above all other things—is forced to a novel conclusion. He cannot accept, on the one hand,

[1] This might be intended as a criticism of Xenophanes (cf. fr. 25, fr. 26), but more probably it is only the next stage in the argument. If νοῦς, then κίνησις.

[2] Reading ὄντων τῶν ὄντων (sc. ὄντως) with Heindorf. Badham reads ὄντων πάντων (cf. πάντα 249 b 8 *infr.*). Neither conjecture seems indispensable.

the view of the Whole of True Being as static—the view alike of those who believe in one Form and those who believe in many. Nor, on the other hand, can he listen for a moment to those who teach universal motion. He must be like the children who ask for "both please" in dealing with everything in the universe moving and unmoved; he must teach that the Whole of True Being is "both".

This passage has suffered much conflicting interpretation. Most scholars have seen in it a direct and drastic modification[1] in Plato's conception of the Forms. But though the *Philebus* might seem to countenance this, any such theory is wrecked by the re-appearance of the Forms in the *Timaeus*[2] evidently quite unmodified. Yet our passage certainly means to claim for κίνησις καὶ ζωὴ καὶ ψυχὴ καὶ φρόνησις a new place within τὸ παντελῶς ὄν. This claim is not to be met by the grudging concession that there is in a sense a case of ποιεῖν καὶ πάσχειν in the act of knowing. As we have seen, that was perhaps the concession the Eleatic Stranger sought to extract from the friends of the Forms in order to bring them a little nearer the "reformed" materialists,[3] but this concession is swallowed up at once in a much wider claim. The activities of soul are not confined to the act of knowing, and a place for it must now be found within τὸ παντελῶς ὄν and alongside the Forms: the Forms are no longer the whole of "True Being". This is perhaps as significant an advance

[1] Cf. L. Rougier (art. "La correspondance des Genres du Sophiste du Philèbe et du Timée", *Archiv für Gesch. der Phil.* XXVII, pp. 365 sqq.): "Cette exclamation (248 e) est prise par la majorité des critiques comme l'annonce d'un changement radical dans la théorie des idées. Après les avoir déclarées immobiles et immuables Platon leur accorde le mouvement, la vie et la pensée. Elles deviennent semblables aux λόγοι de Philon le Juif, des forces intelligentes et actives."

[2] *Tim.* 51 c, d.

[3] *Sophistes* 248 c. This interpretation of the passage is stated by M. Rodier (*Année Philosophique*, vol. XVI, pp. 64, 65): "De même par mouvement, vie et pensée il ne faut pas entendre ici ce que nous désignons ordinairement par ces mots. Les quatre expressions κίνησις καὶ ζωὴ καὶ ψυχὴ καὶ φρόνησις sont équivalentes. La preuve en est que Platon ne parle dans la suite que de mouvement, κίνησις, qu'il prend par substitut des trois autres. Mais de quel mouvement peut-il être question? Sans aucun doute d'un mouvement purement logique, de celui que l'objet accomplit pour se refléter dans le sujet."

as the discovery of the Form of Otherness. The Pythagoreans had admitted plurality in defiance of Parmenides into the world of Forms, but they had never speculated on the internal relations of that world and they had never tampered with the "sign" of immobility which Parmenides had set up. At this point Plato challenges it in order to vindicate the absolute reality of that active principle which he has called τὸ ἑαυτὸ κινοῦν in the *Phaedrus*—it has become "life, soul and understanding" in our passage. The relations of νοῦς and ψυχή and the functions of both in the totality of things are for the moment reserved questions. What has been achieved is simply the recognition that the Forms do not explain the dialectician who studies them, and that therefore some more comprehensive metaphysic is needed to embrace them both. So to state the question is, of course, crude and naive from a neo-Platonic point of view: but if we go back to the *Sophistes* itself and examine it in its context, is it safe to find a more elaborate metaphysic there? Is not this an advance on anything that had gone before?

There is, however, an objection to meet which seems to rise from the *Sophistes* itself. If κίνησις in this sense is to be regarded as real but other than all the Forms, why do we find Forms of κίνησις and στάσις among the μέγιστα γένη of the subsequent argument? On the interpretation of the μέγιστα γένη as *summa genera* this objection might seem insuperable, but once we have accepted Cornford's interpretation[1] of them as "very important Forms", selected partly because we have been discussing κίνησις, partly because they are incompatible opposites covering together the totality of things (while Same and Other are both compatible and all-pervading), we see our way to a possible explanation; and this explanation becomes probable when we take into account the discussion of false speaking and thinking still later in the *Sophistes*.[2] In the course of that discussion we have to examine what happens when we say "Theaetetus flies" of a Theaetetus who is in fact sitting. This is the problem which the figures of the seal and the birdcage in the *Theaetetus* had essayed to solve, but unsuccessfully, since the Forms were there excluded

[1] *Plato's Theory of Knowledge*, pp. 274–278.
[2] *Sophistes* 259d–264d.

from consideration. Now, however, they are brought in. There is a Form of Sitting and a Form of Flying. There is no Form of Theaetetus,[1] but Theaetetus can participate in either Form, and false judgment is to assert the participation which is not in fact taking place. This assumption of Forms corresponding to active and passive verbs strikes us as strange and difficult. Yet if we may trust the Seventh Epistle at all, we must accept περὶ ποιήματα καὶ παθήματα σύμπαντα at the close of the list of the Forms Plato recognised at the end of his life.[2] How then is this to be reconciled with the claim that soul and its activities are outside the scope of the Forms?

It is worth noticing, first of all, that even in the list in the Seventh Epistle we find forms of ζῷα and of ἤθη ἐν ψυχαῖς but none of ψυχαί. This is not perhaps as captious a point as it might at first appear to be, for it marks distinctly the limit of the capacity of the Forms doctrine to express the totality of things, and it marks this as clearly as the *Sophistes* itself. Natural species, types of character *and types of activity* are all patterns, the stamp of which may be set upon any given manifestation of that κίνησις which is also to be defined as ζωὴ καὶ φρόνησις. But this κίνησις itself is other than them all, and yet as real as they. The αὐτόζῳον in the *Timaeus* is not to be identified with the world-soul;[3] neither, then, is the Form of any species to be identified with the ψυχή of any or of all of its members. Similarly the Forms of determinate modes of action and passion are not to be identified with the experiencing subject. This subject is something "truly" real. It has the "true" reality that elevates it above the world of becoming. It has a control over the random motions analogous to that of the world-soul itself: it is an active force as contrasted with the ὑποδοχή which can only receive passively εἰσιόντα καὶ ἐξιόντα τῶν ἀεὶ ὄντων μιμήματα. In fact it governs to some extent this ἐξιέναι and εἰσιέναι if Plutarch's filling out of Plato's meaning be admissible.[4]

Thus to acknowledge Forms of Flying, Sitting, and Man does not

---

[1] Cornford, *Plato's Theory of Knowledge*, p. 314.
[2] *Ep.* VII 342a sqq., esp. d *fin.*
[3] One is bound to anticipate the *Timaeus* in this discussion.
[4] *De Animae Procr.* 1024c; *v. supr.* p. xiv, *infr.* p. 106.

necessitate the acknowledgment of a Form of Theaetetus. Nor does the recognition of "pervading" Forms of Motion and Rest imply that the self-moving soul can be subsumed beneath them so as to lose its distinct essence and power as the αἰτία κινήσεως. The *Sophistes* leaves us with Forms on the one hand (Man, Motion, Rest, Doing, Suffering) and life, mind and soul, which can be called collectively κίνησις, on the other. Like the children, we must ask for both. Both are "truly real". Not all κίνησις is truly real: spatial motion is not. We reach a finding of double significance. κίνησις can be used of non-spatial activity as manifested by a ψυχή. This κίνησις exists within the confines of "True Being". The subsequent domination of Aristotle makes it necessary to lay all possible stress on this use by Plato of the term κίνησις. It is other than the Forms but as real as they, and shares their elevation above the phantasmagoria of becoming. "True Being" is more than the Forms.

The *Sophistes* also gives us an interesting passage in which the "demiurgic" work of God is distinguished from the workings of φύσις ἄνευ διανοίας.[1] This passage is rather incidental to the main theme of the dialogue and the Eleatic Stranger is being pious rather than dialectical at this point: its interest is in its preparing us for the serious attempt in the *Timaeus* to give a physical and cosmological account of the working of the divine artificer and the random spirit of the world untamed. Here they are stated in opposition: in the *Politicus* we shall find them brought closely together. Only in the *Timaeus* are they "causes" whose working can be traced in detail in the οὐρανός.

(f) The Politicus

The *Politicus* has an importance for our subject both as a whole and in its myth of the age of Cronos in particular. The neglect which the *Laws* has suffered in England until recently has been and still is the lot of the *Politicus*, though Lewis Campbell left us in no doubt of its importance in his edition of 1867. Writing after Syracuse and in one of his critical dialogues, Plato still clings to the figure of the philosopher-king who appears as the one wise ruler, who can be

[1] *Sophistes* 265 c sqq.

above law and modify law because he is master of the art of government and has in himself the vitality and insight to sustain the state.
This marked reluctance in the *Politicus* to admit the domination
of the fixed system of law, which is allowed only as a *pis aller*,
contrasts forcibly with the perfunctory admission in the *Laws* that
a ruler who is "above the law" is ideally possible.[1] We cannot tell
whether in the *Philosophus* Plato would have brought together the
διαλεκτικός from the *Sophistes* and the wise shepherd of the flock[2]
from the *Politicus* and united them in the person of the philosopher,
contrasting him with sophists and politicians alike; but this is at
least a fusion which, on the evidence of both dialogues, one must
admit to be κατὰ φύσιν.

The direct bearing of this on the question of κίνησις lies in its
elucidation of the wider, non-spatial senses of the word in which,
as we have seen, Plato came to use it by the time of his writing the
Sophistes. The development of the idea of a δημιουργός from Socratic
beginnings will concern us later, but the constant Platonic principle
of the royal rule of νοῦς underlies the *Politicus* as surely as the
Republic. But since the *Sophistes* has been written, this must have
a deeper metaphysical significance which will only come to full
expression in the *Philebus*, but which is none the less there all the
time. Its most notable outcrop is in the myth, but we must not ignore
its presence underground in the rest of the dialogue.

In turning to the *Politicus* myth we need to heed Campbell's
kindly warning that "the harmonist of Plato's myths would have
a task only less difficult than the rationalist of the old mythology—
ἅτε ἀγροικῷ τινι σοφίᾳ χρώμενος, πολλῆς αὐτῷ σχολῆς δεήσει".[3] One
who sets out to harmonise the story of Atlantis or the myth in the
Protagoras with the *Politicus* myth would ask for this condemnation,
but it may not be so fruitless for us to seek certain cosmological
principles which have been hinted at previously in non-mythical

---

[1] *Politicus* 295 b sqq.; *Laws* IX 875 a. Campbell, Introduction to *Politicus*,
pp. xv, xvi.
[2] This may be said to hold good in spite of the distinction drawn between
divine νομεύς and human ἐπιμελητής at 276 d.
[3] *Plato, Sophistes and Politicus: Politicus*, Intro. p. xxxii.

passages and which reappear in the *Timaeus* and in the tenth book of the *Laws*. Plato could not write his *Politicus* myth in complete detachment from the astronomical and cosmological ideas which had been gradually increasing their hold upon him; and, after all, in a dialogue planned as the *Politicus* must be there is no means as apt as a myth of indicating the *Weltbild* implied in it. The mythology and the reminiscences of the early cosmogonies are significant enough because they seem to be selected artificially to carry the fundamental cosmological ideas to an extent that we do not find, for instance, in the myth of Er or in the *Protagoras* myth. One passage may be considered as bringing these fundamental ideas to light and expressing them in a form that is almost λόγος:[1]

Ever to abide in the same relation and the same condition is the privilege of the divinest of all things alone: the nature of the bodily does not entitle it to this rank. Now the Heaven, or Universe, as we have chosen to call it, has received many blessed gifts from him who brought it into being, but it has also been made to partake in bodily form. Therefore it is impossible for it to be free from change altogether, and yet so far as may be it is moved with one motion and as nearly as possible in the same place and keeping the same relations. For this reason it has received its reversal of motion, for this is the least possible distortion of its proper[2] motion. But to revolve ever by his own power is possible only to the lord and leader of all things that move; for him to change from one direction of motion to another would flout Heaven's law. It follows from all this that we must not say of this Universe either that it revolves ever by its own power, or that it is ever and completely under God's power and yet receives two contrary revolutions from His impulse, or, again, that there are two gods at contrary purposes which reveal themselves in its contrary revolutions: we must assert the only remaining possibility, as we did just now, and say that at times it is assisted on its way by the transcendent divine cause, gaining life once again and an immortality renewed from its Artificer, while in the other periods when it is left to itself it revolves under its own power and, when it is released, it has by that time gathered such force

---

[1] *Politicus* 269 d sqq.
[2] Campbell would read ταὐτοῦ. But this misses the point that the ἀνακύκλησις, though the "salvation" of the οὐρανός, is strictly a παράλλαξις of its natural motion imposed by God. The first two sentences of 269 e refer to this natural motion of the οὐρανός.

that it revolves in the reverse sense for tens of thousands of revolutions[1] because its size is so great, its balance so perfect and the pivot upon which it turns so small.

In the *Phaedrus* proof of immortality we found the fusion of Ionian ἀρχή and Orphic ψυχή under the form of τὸ ἑαυτὸ κινοῦν. We recognised that the argument was a forerunner of the "cosmological argument" rather than of the "ontological". Without ψυχή, the οὐρανός and all the γένεσις within it must collapse and cease. But we were not considering specifically the soul of the οὐρανός at that point: Plato was content with the generalisation that all soul tends and moves all body; and an attempt at a direct astronomical application of this to the details of the myth we chose to discount.[2] In the *Sophistes*, moreover, we were dealing with the metaphysical "dignity" of κίνησις, its claim to be ὄντως ὄν in the form of ψυχὴ καὶ ζωὴ καὶ φρόνησις. Now we come to a rather suspiciously reasoned myth which not only anticipates the *Timaeus* in many details, but is at one with that dialogue and with the *Laws* in certain more fundamental assumptions. We have now to add to our fusion of ἀρχή and ψυχή another union—that of the Pythagorean οὐρανός[3] with the One of Parmenides.[4] We have also to recognise another active power. This agent we might have regarded as impersonal had the passage finished at 269e 5; but we find it becoming an evidently personal agency, and named God and Artificer, as the argument proceeds. This δημιουργός[5] transcends the οὐρανός; he has nothing created or bodily in him, for he is able to perform the constant single revolution which the οὐρανός cannot perform simply because it is bodily and created. He must not be credited with cross-

---

[1] The περίοδοι are daily revolutions of the οὐρανός. The last sentences appear to give an explanation on mechanical grounds (cf. the humming-tops (στρόβιλοι) which seem to have been in Plato's mind here as at *Rep.* 436). This would be inconsistent with the theory of psychic impulse if regarded as an exhaustive explanation.

[2] P. 5 *supr.*

[3] In the third sense of Ar. *De Caelo* A 9, 278 b 20, meaning "the heaven and all it contains".

[4] Also, perhaps, with the One of Melissus.

[5] At 273 b *init.* we find δημιουργοῦ καὶ πατρός, the *Timaeus* phrase.

purposes, so as to be the cause of good and evil at once—that is to say of both of the motions exhibited by the οὐρανός; nor has he an equal divine antagonist: the return of the οὐρανός to the sense of motion natural to it is due to the dictate of its own soul—though this is ultimately subject to its creator and preserved by his intervention.

We are told two things concerning the οὐρανός—that it is a ζῷον, and that it lacks perfection because it is an embodied creature. It might seem that we had here a reassertion of the *Phaedo* position, that in changeless (and therefore motionless) being alone is perfection; but now we find an important modification. The perfection the embodied οὐρανός fails to attain is now ascribed τῷ τῶν κινουμένων αὖ πάντων ἡγουμένῳ.[1] This "Leader of all things that move" must be the same as the θεός and the δημιουργός of the following sentences. His prerogative, it appears, consists in constant self-motion in the form of rotation in one sense (αὐτὸ ἑαυτὸ στρέφειν ἀεί). We have here two developments of the *Phaedrus* position. The κίνησις has become στρέφειν: this στρέφειν, however, is not in space at all, for the "Leader" in whom it is found is distinguished from the οὐρανός in that he is not a creature with a body. Secondly, there is a complication of the "cosmological argument". The observed facts demand a world-soul admittedly, but they do not reveal a perfect rotation. We must therefore posit a first mover who exhibits that constant activity which though not spatial is to be described as αὐτὸ ἑαυτὸ στρέφειν ἀεί, and only in the second place a derived (and not entirely obedient and constant) world-soul that is directly responsible for the external motions in space.

We come, then, to the irregularities of the οὐρανός and to the notion of ἀνακύκλησις. It might seem at first that this is of no help in extracting the residue of significant cosmological teaching from

[1] Campbell (*ad loc.*) says that "αὖ implies a contrast between the divinest of all things and the leader of all that is in motion", and by the latter he understands, according to the later part of the same note, Pure Soul or God. If by this he means that Pure Soul does not belong to the class of the θειότατα, this seems difficult; that class surely includes Forms and "Leader". If so, αὖ would rather express the contrast between him and all lesser movers.

the myth, since the ἀνακύκλησις might appear to be demanded only by the historical (or rather prehistoric) details. Yet the history is, after all, as closely related to the cosmology as in the poem of Empedocles. In the eighth and ninth books of the *Republic* the progressive decadence of men and states is related to the universe only in the designedly mysterious remarks about the number of the period of the human creature. Men decline by reason of ethical failures shown in successive acts of disobedience to "man's best guardian, reason conjoined with music".[1] In the *Politicus* myth, however, human life is made to depend on the vicissitudes of the cosmos.[2] This is not so much a relapse into more primitive conceptions as a considered attribution of ethical meaning to cosmological events. The moral conflict in the soul of the οὐρανός is reflected in every form of γένεσις within it: the refusal to be guided by the "leader of all things that move" brings about the periods of lawlessness and disruption. Therefore Plutarch's parallel[3] between the εἱμαρμένη καὶ σύμφυτος ἐπιθυμία of this dialogue[4] and the so-called "evil world-soul" of the *Laws*, though obviously wrong, and contradicted explicitly by Plato himself in so far as it implies a Zoroastrian dualism,[5] is nevertheless right in so far as it implies an ethical as well as a physical relapse in the return of the οὐρανός to its "automatic" course.

Plutarch tries also to equate the σύμφυτος ἐπιθυμία with the ἀπειρία of the *Philebus*. This we can set aside. But what of the identification with ἀνάγκη in the *Timaeus?* The word seems to be used in a sense which is half physical in the sentence immediately before the passage we have translated: our passage is the Stranger's answer to the request of Young Socrates for an explanation of this sentence.[6] Yet there are two points of difference. In the first place, we do not

---

[1] *Rep.* VIII 549b 6. See Taylor's article in *Mind*, XLVIII, pp. 23–30.

[2] ᾧ συμμιμούμενοι καὶ συνεπόμενοι, νῦν μὲν οὕτως τότε δὲ ἐκείνως ζῶμέν τε καὶ φυόμεθα, 274d *fin.*

[3] Plut. *De Animae Procr. in Timaeo* 1014d sqq.

[4] 272e.

[5] μήτε αὖ δύο τινὲ θεώ, κ.τ.λ., 270a *init.*

[6] ΞΕ. τοῦτο δ' αὐτῷ τὸ ἀνάπαλιν ἰέναι. διὰ τόδ' ἐξ ἀνάγκης ἔμφυτον γέγονεν. ΝΕ. ΣΩ. διὰ τὸ ποῖον δή; 269d.

find it clearly stated that the cause of disorder is a psychic force working in the bodily realm rather than the fact of being embodied. The *Politicus* myth in this keeps close to the digression in the *Theaetetus*,[1] and the *Timaeus* marks the first clear statement to the contrary in cosmological terms, though we have the point made in the *Philebus* that so-called bodily desires really arise from the soul. In the second place, the actual motion allowed to the σύμφυτος ἐπιθυμία is a rotation. In the *Timaeus* this would be impossible, and it is at this point that we have to admit that our passage is deliberately constructed to fit the story and to give it a cosmic background; for even the myth of Er is more "likely"[2] astronomically than this. Yet though this dramatic sequence of revolution and counter-revolution becomes in the *Timaeus* a constant undercurrent of opposition by ἀνάγκη to the forces of reason revealed in rotation, the part played by the two forces, σύμφυτος ἐπιθυμία in the *Politicus* and ἀνάγκη in the *Timaeus*, is sufficiently similar for the one to throw light on the other. The former belongs to a mere story: the latter, we shall argue, is the best account reason can give of the forces of unreason and their work in the visible universe.

(g) The Philebus

We have remarked already on the point made in the analysis of ἐπιθυμία in the *Philebus* that all desire is of the soul and that, strictly speaking, no bodily desire exists.[3] Apart from this, we have only to consider what light the fourfold classification of πάντα τὰ νῦν ὄντα ἐν τῷ παντί[4] throws on the development of Plato's doctrine of κίνησις. Fortunately this is less obscure than the relation of this passage to the Forms doctrine, either as it appears in the dialogues or as Aristotle states it; but we must begin from a general consideration of the passage. Taylor has pointed out that "the fourfold classification has been devised with a view to a problem where the

---

[1] Cf. *Theaet.* 176a: τόνδε τὸν τόπον περιπολεῖ ἐξ ἀνάγκης. *Politicus* 273b: τούτων δ' αὐτῷ τὸ σωματοειδὲς τῆς συγκράσεως αἴτιον.
[2] On the εἰκὼς λόγος, *v. infr.* p. 67.
[3] *Philebus* 34e sqq. This is to be contrasted with *Rep.* IX 585b sqq.
[4] *Philebus* 23c sqq.

forms are not specially relevant",[1] the problem of the relative "reality" of ἡδονή and νοῦς.[2] This "placing" of νοῦς therefore has a direct interest for us, though we are not so concerned with its competition with ἡδονή for an ethical "second prize".

Plato begins by taking the "whole of reality" for analysis, and there seems to be some reason other than an artistic one for adding a third class to πέρας and ἄπειρον at once without apology, then a fourth after apology, then a half jocular suggestion of a fifth. It would seem that the divine revelation which came by Pythagoras had taught men of πέρας and ἄπειρον, from which the "mixed" class could be at once deduced, but that the fourth is something that goes beyond Pythagoreanism, is, in fact, that which combines the work of the φιλία of Empedocles and of the νοῦς of Anaxagoras. The fifth factor, that "may prove necessary", is perhaps that which corresponds to the νεῖκος of Empedocles, as Bury says: Plato, at any rate, calls it διάκρισιν δυνάμενόν τι.[3] The question of its "necessity" is partly the question of its relevance to the matter under discussion. Plato may be hinting that if we were not merely "placing" νοῦς and ἡδονή, but were really giving an account of the totality of things, a psychic force other than νοῦς would have to be recognised. It is not impossible, in Plato, for a joke of Protarchus to mean so much.

We come next to a study of the αἰτία τῆς μίξεως itself, and consider what μίξις here involves. Jackson's view—that we have described in the passage two operations in which πέρας limits ἄπειρον, the evolution of the Forms themselves and the creation of natural objects—is difficult to sustain in view of the fact that we have no hint of this in the description of μικτά, which are all taken from the world of "events".[4] The significant thing is the description of these

---

[1] A. E. Taylor, *Plato, the Man and his Work*, p. 417: recent discussions mentioned *ib.* n. 1.
[2] Raeder's summary of the solution Plato reaches is: "Also: die Lust ist unbegrenzt, wird aber im Gemischten verwirklicht; die Vernunft ist Ursache der Mischung, verwirklicht aber die Lust im Gemischten dadurch, dass sie die Begrenzung ins Unbegrenzte einführt" (*Platons philosophische Entwickelung*, p. 370).
[3] *Philebus* 23 d *fin.*; cf. R. G. Bury, *The Philebus of Plato*, ad loc.
[4] Taylor, *Plato, the Man and his Work*, p. 417.

natural states and objects as γεγενημένη οὐσία and of their creation as γένεσις εἰς οὐσίαν: it is better to regard this as a new valuation of the natural order[1] than to insist that οὐσία must imply that we are dealing with the Forms. Therefore any professedly neo-Platonic interpretation of the αἰτία τῆς μίξεως which regards νοῦς as an agent in the determination of the Forms[2] is unsupported by this passage, and we can limit our attention to the μίξις which brings about the comparative permanence and stability of the embodiments of the Forms in the οὐρανός—precisely the work of νοῦς as δημιουργός in the *Timaeus*. But if the *Philebus* is "metaphysic", can we set down the identical statement in the *Timaeus* as "mere cosmology"? Moreover, we find here in the *Philebus* that the fourth class, the αἰτία, is as unquestionably part of the "totality of real things" as are πέρας and ἄπειρον. The extension of the boundary of what is to be recognised as real lies here in the recognition of the third class, that of μικτά, as possessing γεγενημένη οὐσία.

There are other points in the account of the αἰτία which relate it both to the *Sophistes* passage we have already discussed and to the *Timaeus*. In all three we are told that νοῦς is only to be found in a ψυχή, a dogma which we shall have to consider in our attempt to summarise Plato's view of the ultimate ἀρχὴ κινήσεως.[3] The glorification of νοῦς βασιλεύς, however, is not allowed to contravene this dogma. But the terms of the ἐγκώμιον are interesting. The "elements" in terrestrial creatures and the souls that govern them are said to be less pure than the divine mind and pure elements of the οὐρανός, here named Zeus. Yet it is one and the same αἰτία manifesting itself in all and governing all. It is the fount of vigour and of healing. It sets in order years, seasons, and months. This appeal from microcosm to macrocosm implies that it is the function

---

[1] On this point I follow Natorp ("Es ist sehr zu beachten, dass hiermit, zum ersten Mal in dieser Deutlichkeit, das Werden einen ganz positiven Sinn erlangt", *Platos Ideenlehre* (ed. 1903), p. 308 *fin.*), but not in his interpretation of αἰτία.

[2] The discussion in Plotinus, *Enn.* VI, VII 25 (*v.* VI, VII *passim*), does not seem to take it so.

[3] *Sophistes* 249a 4; *Philebus* 30a 9; *Timaeus* 30b 3. Ch. VIII *infr.* We also note the equating of αἰτία, ποιοῦν and δημιουργοῦν *Phileb.* 27a sqq.

of νοῦς in the οὐρανός that is all-important, even in a question concerning the good for man.

Our tracing of Plato's thought on what Aristotle was to call the αἰτία ἦ ἀρχὴ κινήσεως has brought us as far as the *Timaeus*. To estimate the validity of this dialogue as evidence for Plato's later theory of motion, we need to keep in mind all that has gone before it in the earlier dialogues. But we must also consider briefly some of the pre-Socratic sources on which Plato relied in parts of the *Timaeus*. In doing so, we are not committing ourselves to any particular theory of the dialogue as a whole; that can only be attempted when the materials for a judgment have been assembled.

CHAPTER II

IONIAN ELEMENTS IN THE *TIMAEUS*

Plato's direct obligations to the Ionians in the *Timaeus* seem at first sight to be negligible, and to justify Taylor's contention, as far as the "matter" of the dialogue is concerned, that we have in it a fusion of Empedoclean biology and Pythagorean mathematics.[1] Yet the development we have traced so far of the incorporation of Ionian as well as Orphic ideas into Plato's view of the "totality of the real" does not halt abruptly on the threshold of the *Timaeus*, but is fully accepted and used in it; and we have only to ask ourselves whether the dialogue could have been what it is if Plato had never heard of the νοῦς of Anaxagoras, to see that the eastern tradition is drawn upon as well as the western and that we have in the *Timaeus* no period-piece keeping strictly to dramatic proprieties. Yet it must be admitted that what Plato draws from the Ionians in the *Timaeus* itself is slight: he rather takes over from the *Philebus*, the *Phaedrus* and the *Cratylus* the Ionian ideas he had already incorporated into his thought. We must therefore expect somewhat negative results if we examine the *Timaeus* for distinct "traces" of individual Ionian thinkers.

In the case of the Milesians, for example, the ideas that can be regarded as taken over in any sense are just the points that are not distinctively Ionian. If Anaximander's use of ἄπειρον does indicate something alarmingly like the ultimate curvature of space, as has been recently contended,[2] this makes Anaximander anticipate the closed οὐρανός of the Pythagoreans rather than the innumerable atom-worlds in the absolute void of the Atomists, which was, after all, the Ionian doctrine. His "cart-wheel" orbits of sun, moon and stars only reappear in Plato after they have been modified and so adapted to the Pythagorean double-motion astronomy. Similarly

[1] A. E. Taylor, *A Commentary on Plato's Timaeus*, p. 11.
[2] F. M. Cornford, "The Invention of Space", in *Essays in Honour of Gilbert Murray* (London, 1936).

Anaximenes's description of the stars as set in a sphere, and the distinction between stars and planets which Sir Thomas Heath believes to be involved in this[1] passed over into the western systems and were neglected by the subsequent Ionians.

Thus it is in the concept of the ἀρχή itself, the "ageless and deathless", that we find the common element of the Ionians which Plato took up, as the "etymology" of δίκαιον in the *Cratylus* shows.[2] We have already hinted at the distinction between Heraclitus himself and the Heracliteans of Plato's own time. Karl Reinhardt's *dictum* that Plato knew Heraclitus only through the Heracliteans[3] is contradicted by the evidence of the dialogues themselves.[4] But Plato does perhaps make a sharper distinction than the original warranted, conceding the materialist side wholly to the Heracliteans and following Heraclitus in such doctrines as the ἀνταπόδοσις of the *Phaedo*,[5] and an important section of the speech of Diotima.[6] Thus while the *Timaeus* account of the motion of physical bodies accepts the Heraclitean position as far as sheer mechanical κίνησις is concerned, and more particularly in regard to the ἐπίρρυτον καὶ ἀπόρρυτον σῶμα[7] of the mortal creature, Heraclitus's account of the ever-living fire which is λόγος and σοφία is not adequate in itself to describe the psychic forces which govern the bodily motions. The soul now has its περίοδοι, which show the influence of the Pythagorean οὐρανός.

In the system of Anaxagoras we need concern ourselves only with

---

[1] Aëtius II 14, 3 (Diels, *Dox. Gr.* p. 344); Heath, *Aristarchus*, pp. 40 sqq.; Tannery, *Pour l'histoire de la science hellène*, p. 154.

[2] *Crat.* 411a sqq.; *v.* p. 2 *supr.*

[3] *Parmenides und die Geschichte der griechischen Philosophie* (Bonn, 1916), p. 291.

[4] Cf. Campbell, Introduction to *Theaetetus*, p. xliv: "It is not surprising therefore if Plato grasped the thought of Heraclitus more firmly than his own followers had done." Heraclitus's book survived (Ar. *Rhet.* Γ 5, 1407b 11) and found ἐξηγηταί (D.L. IX i 11). The reference to the "sun of Heraclitus" at *Rep.* 498a *fin.* implies familiarity with the antiquated astronomical ideas of Heraclitus himself. The Heracliteans perhaps believed the sun to be new every instant, but hardly that it was new every morning.

[5] 70d 7–72c 2.

[6] *Symp.* 207d. Contrast *Theaet.* 159a, which is "Heraclitean".

[7] *Tim.* 42a sqq.

νοῦς. The point at which Anaxagoras is nearer Plato and further from Heraclitus and from all the lesser Ionians is in his making νοῦς to be not only κρατῶν but also ἀμιγής. Whether he may be called "the first decisive and conscious dualist among Greek philosophers" as Rohde names him[1] is doubtful, quite apart from our interpretation of Parmenides. But the clear distinction of νοῦς from the περιχώρησις it sets up is a decisive step towards the πρωτουργοὶ καὶ δευτερουργοὶ κινήσεις of Plato's *Laws*.

But is the νοῦς of Anaxagoras conceived as moving? Aristotle tried to make it out to be an unmoved mover as well as an "unmixed" knower.[2] But the whole significance of νοῦς is surely that while it is λεπτότατον—distinct, at least, from the bodies it "governs"—its essence is to be mobile. It keeps the κράτος, ἰσχύς, γνώμη[3] that Heraclitus gave to fire, but loses the material side. There is perhaps no better summary of its meaning than the one Plato gives in the *Cratylus*:[4] αὐτοκράτορα γὰρ αὐτὸν ὄντα καὶ οὐδενὶ μεμιγμένον, πάντα φησὶν αὐτὸν κοσμεῖν...διὰ πάντων ἰόντα. This νοῦς is no absentee Deist God who only initiated the unfolding of the world; νοῦς governs all things and many things have a portion of it, though it is always unmixed.[5] This could not be said of that which gave an original impulse and then dissociated itself from what it had impelled. This misconception of νοῦς really goes back to the famous *Phaedo*

---

[1] *Psyche*, Eng. tr. p. 386 *fin.*

[2] Ar. *De Anima* 404a 25, 429a 15 sqq. (cf. Trendelenburg *ad loc.*: "Aristoteles, cum cognoscendi naturam propositam haberet, quae universa quadam imagine significata latius patuisse videntur ad solam cognitionem traxit"), also *Phys.* Θ 5, 256b 24. Burnet (*E. G. Ph.*[3] p. 268 n. 1) makes out that μόνως κινοίη ἀκίνητος ὤν here is "not meant to be historical" while κρατοίη ἀμιγὴς ὤν is so intended! This is to concede to Aristotle a finer historical sense than is usually evident in his treatment of earlier thinkers, and seems to imply a deliberate intention to confuse. The simpler explanation is surely that Aristotle saw that νοῦς approximated to ἐνέργεια rather than to κίνησις in his own system and interpreted Anaxagoras accordingly.

[3] fr. 12 (Diels). ἰσχει here probably has its proper sense and is not a mere synonym for ἔχει. The action of the soul at *Tim.* 37a, b may be compared in essentials with this account of νοῦς, but there the motion is in circles and like knows like.

[4] *Crat.* 413c 5.   [5] fr. 12 (Diels) *init.*

passage, which Aristotle followed in the *Metaphysics*.[1] The passage in the *Apology*,[2] if considered together with them both, probably reflects the bad name Anaxagoras and his followers had gained at Athens by their "impious" astronomy: it does not prove that Anaxagoras did in fact abandon νοῦς and resort to mechanical explanations alone, and the fragments testify the opposite. As Plato turned from the Heracliteans without failing to understand and use the work of Heraclitus, so his deeper revulsion from Archelaus did not prevent his accepting and incorporating into his own thought the νοῦς of Anaxagoras. His νοῦς κοσμοποιός is, of course, of first importance for an understanding of the Δημιουργός of the *Timaeus*.

Cicero tells us that Democritus said "I came to Athens and no one knew me"[3] and Valerius Maximus enlarges on this statement.[4] While this tradition is in no way decisive, one must look for strong argument to the contrary if disproof of it is to depend on internal evidence of the dialogues alone. In the case of the *Timaeus* this has been sought of late by two German scholars, encouraged by the judgments of Archer Hind and of Natorp. Frau Hammer-Jensen[5] believed that the abrupt break at 46e implied that Plato had at that point become aware of Democritean atomism and answered it in the next twenty pages of the dialogue. Eva Sachs claimed that Plato shows a knowledge of Atomism, which he criticises from a Pythagorean point of view and with the help of Theaetetus's work in stereometry. This is not the place to discuss these claims. Apelt points out in his note on the passage that the strictly mathematical character of the discussion of the elementary triangles tells against Eva Sachs's contentions, and shows that there is really no influence so strong there as that of Theaetetus. On the general issue of "mechanism" and materialism, there is no need to suppose that the Atomists are being criticised. Mr Tate has shown recently[7]

---

[1] *Phaedo* 98 b 7 sqq.; *Metaph.* A 4, 985 a 18.   [2] *Ap. Socr.* 26c, d.
[3] *Tusc. Disp.* v 36, 104; cf. D.L. ix 36.
[4] Diels, *F. d. V.*[5] 68 A 11.
[5] I. Hammer-Jensen, 'Demokrit und Platon', *Archiv für Gesch. der Phil.* Band xxiii (1910).
[6] E. Sachs, *Die fünf platonischen Körper* (Berlin, 1917), esp. pp. 187 sqq.
[7] *Class. Quart.* xxx, pp. 48 sqq.; *Laws* x 889e sqq.

that the materialists of *Laws* x are more probably followers of Archelaus than of Empedocles or Democritus. Such Ἀναξαγόρειοι are mentioned in the Διссοὶ Λόγοι[1] and by Plato himself in the *Cratylus*. Together with the various Heraclitean factions[2] they seem to represent the "crass" materialism that Plato regarded as his natural enemy.

As far as κίνησις on its mechanical side is concerned, we have seen that Plato had already made a complete dichotomy of the hylozoist ἀρχή into psychic and physical movents. The ῥᾳθυμία with which Aristotle charges the Atomists[3] consists, no doubt, in their refusal to allot a psychic cause to motion or to hold a doctrine of "natural motions" of the simple bodies. Plato, however, proceeding from his own principles, had arrived, as we shall see, at a classification of derived (that is "bodily") motions that the Atomists never achieved. He would say they never got beyond the ninth of his ten "kinds" in the *Laws* classification, and their doctrine of κίνησις would have nothing new or interesting in it for him, whatever may be the truth concerning his familiarity with their doctrine of atoms and void.

[1] Δ. Λ. vi 8; 6, 8. *F. d. V.*[5] 90, vol. ii, p. 414; *Crat.* 409 b.
[2] Cf. *Theaet.* 179 d sqq. Professor Cornford points out to me that Aristotle could inform Plato of the Atomist systems, and no doubt did so. Undoubtedly, but this is not evidence to support Frau Hammer-Jensen in her contention, and one cannot suppose that Plato would be interested in their view of motion.
[3] Ar. *Metaph.* A 4, 985 b 19.

CHAPTER III

ANTECEDENTS OF THE ΚΙΝΗΣΙΣ-DOCTRINE OF THE *TIMAEUS* IN ALCMAEON, THE PYTHAGOREANS AND THE MEDICAL WRITERS

A consideration of all the Pythagorean elements in the *Timaeus* would take us beyond our present question. We may remark, however, that the word "Pythagorean" can be used to cover much that ought rather to be called "Western". We shall consider later the factors that seem to come through Empedocles directly from an Orphic background with no obvious relation to the Pythagorean school: for the doctrine of κίνησις these are more important than anything unmistakably Pythagorean. Moreover, in the uncertainty and conflict of testimony as to what can be attributed to the first two generations of the school and what to a fourth-century Pythagoreanism already in close touch with the Academy, we may look for a guiding thread in the well-attested evidence concerning one thinker, whose work Plato seems to have used to a remarkable extent in the *Timaeus*, Alcmaeon of Croton. He is unquestionably "early", and when we find certain assumptions implied in his sayings we may reasonably claim that if these same assumptions are made by Plato in the *Timaeus*, Plato was accepting principles and doctrines that belonged to the early Pythagorean tradition, though he, like Alcmaeon, was making his own use of them.

According to Aristotle, Alcmaeon was a contemporary of the old age of Pythagoras.[1] We are not told explicitly that he belonged to

---

[1] *Metaph.* A 5, 986a 29 sqq. Ross, *ad loc.*, seems to support Brandis and Zeller in doubting καὶ γάρ...Πυθαγόρᾳ because the words are absent in Aᵇ Al, while arguing that the fact is attested by Iamblichus, *Vit. Pyth.* 104. But in that passage Philolaus and Leucippus are also named as οἱ παλαιότατοι καὶ αὐτῷ συγχρονίσαντες καὶ μαθητεύσαντες τῷ Πυθαγόρᾳ πρεσβύτῃ νέοι and this is obviously unhistorical. Wachtler, whose edition of the fragments is the most recent individual work on them (*De Alcmaeone Crotoniata*, Lipsiae, 1896), defends the reading in Ar. *Metaph.* A.

Wachtler has valuable discussions on the fragments but does not

the Crotoniate medical school, but the fragments themselves put this beyond question. The medical school probably existed before Pythagoras came to Croton: the story of Democedes and the list of Crotoniate victors at Olympia in the first part of the sixth century attest this. There must have been a close relationship between the school and the Brotherhood and no doubt the Pythagorean concern for dietetics, as distinct from religious abstinences, can be traced to this early period. It is to this period Alcmaeon belongs. Burnet in *Early Greek Philosophy* treats of him after Parmenides and so tends to give a false impression of his date: Burnet also tells us that "he accepted Herakleitos's theory of eclipses" as if he were later than Heraclitus too. But we may suppose that he was contemporary with Pythagoras while still at Croton, before his retirement to Metaponton. Pythagoras's death can hardly be later than 496, and Heraclitus (fr. 17 Bywater) and Xenophanes (fr. 7 Diels) speak of him in the past tense. If Chiapelli[1] was right in arguing for a later date for Anaximenes and mutual influence of Pythagoras and Anaximenes upon each other's cosmological ideas, it would be to the early stage in the historical development of Pythagoreanism when this influence was at work that Alcmaeon belongs. Only Iamblichus, Diogenes Laertius and the scholiast on Plato's *First Alcibiades* (121 e) make Alcmaeon definitely a Pythagorean: Simplicius (on Aristotle, *De Anima* 405 a 29), knowing of this view, claims Aristotle's support against it. Cicero, as Krische pointed out,[2] in the indirect doxography in the Epicurean's speech in the first book of the *De Natura Deorum* treats of Alcmaeon before Pythagoras and after the Ionians. A sentence of Martin's sums up the evidence:[3]

Il existait, il est vrai, un ouvrage authentique du médecin Alcmaeon de Croton, qui, plus jeune que Pythagore, fut pourtant contemporain

---

pursue the enquiry "quae ratio intercedat inter Alcmaeonem ceterosque Graecorum medicos et philosophos" beyond Democritus.

A list of recent articles is given by Signorella Luigia Stella, art. "Importanza di Alcmeone nella storia del pensiero greco", *Reale Accademia Nazionale dei Lincei*, Ser. VI, vol. VIII, fasc. IV, p. 244 n. 3. The fragments and evidence are collected in Diels, *F. d. V.*[5] 24.

[1] "Zu Anaximenes und Pythagoras", *Archiv für Gesch. der Phil.* Band I.
[2] *Die theologischen Lehren der griechischen Denker*, p. 68.
[3] Art. "Hypothèse astronomique de Pythagore", *Bullettino di Bibliografia e di Storia delle scienze matematiche e fisiche*, V, p. 100.

du séjour de Pythagore en cette ville; mais Alcmaeon était moins pythagoricien qu'un penseur indépendant qui seulement avait subi l'influence du voisinage de l'école pythagoricienne.

We have to consider what it was in Alcmaeon's work that made Plato in the *Timaeus* so willing to draw upon his findings.

Clearly it was not the doctrine of ἰσονομία in which Alcmaeon stood closest to the Pythagoreans, though this is important as illustrating his tendency to find macrocosmic laws in the microcosm: for this doctrine reads like an application of Anaximander's macrocosmic law (that the opposites pay retribution to one another according to the ordinance of time) to the processes of the microcosm.[1] We may therefore expect a similar analogy in the case of κίνησις and κυκλοφορία. There is no evidence that he wrote more than one book, though this may be no more than the uniform tradition concerning the early thinkers.[2] In any case, however, one would

---

[1] The answer to Aristotle's question whether Alcmaeon derived his "opposite pairs" from the Pythagoreans or they from him is probably that Alcmaeon derived them from Anaximander (fr. 1) but accepted the Pythagorean principle of the limit as being truer than δίκη and χρόνου τάξις. But this explanation by the principle of the limit is doubtful. Wachtler rightly says (*op. cit.* p. 89): "Praeterea numerorum doctrinae, quam Pythagoreorum primarium fuisse placitum scimus, ne minimum quidem in Alcmaeonis fragmentis vestigium extat." Still less is a political reference likely in ἰσονομία (Burnet, *E. G. Ph.* p. 196), for even if Alcmaeon was a Pythagorean, political interests and activity on his part are unlikely; if, however, he were political, it would be on the aristocratic side and ἰσονομία was a democratic catchword (cf. Herodotus III 80; Plato, *Menexenus* 239a).

[2] The actual evidences seem to depend entirely on Aristotle and Theophrastus, unless Chalcidius (*In Tim.* p. 279 Wrobel; Diels 24 A 10) followed an independent medical source. It seems that neither Alcmaeon's book nor Aristotle's Πρὸς τὰ 'Αλκμαίωνος (D.L. v 25) survived in Simplicius's time, though the περὶ φύσεως of Diogenes of Apollonia apparently did (*S. in Phys.* 151, 20). The statement that Alcmaeon was the first to write a φυσικὸς λόγος, made by Clement (*Strom.* 1 78), is difficult, for Anaximander and Anaximenes are earlier, while the tradition reported in D.L. VIII 15, 85 was that Philolaus was the first Pythagorean to publish a work. Tannery suggested (art. "Sur le secret dans l'école de Pythagore", *A.G.P.* 1, p. 34) that Alcmaeon was an ἀκουσματικός publishing contrary to the rule; but in fact he was probably not a Pythagorean at all.

expect some unifying principle in this work, and a complete hiatus between the original work in empirical psychology on the one hand and the sayings concerning the soul on the other is not to be accepted without the strongest evidence. While it is true that the main tenet on the empirical side, that "the brain furnishes the sensations", could have been suggested to Plato by the Coan medical school, it is only in Alcmaeon and in the *Timaeus* that such judgments and findings are found closely linked to what appear to us crude and unscientific descriptions of literal reflection of the motions of the heavenly bodies in the human soul. It is true that we cannot prove conclusively that Alcmaeon taught that there was a kind of orrery in the human brain; but it does seem that this most fantastic conceit of the *Timaeus* can only be a development on *a priori* grounds of some of his ideas, of which the surviving fragments give definite hints, and which no later philosopher or medical man can have taught. These passages are far more primitive than anything Philistion and Archytas could have taught, but it does not follow that they are archaisms introduced, as Taylor would have it, for dramatic reasons. No "Empedoclean biologist" would have countenanced them, and if Plato accepts them so readily there must have been a reason for it: we shall come later to a consideration of what it may have been.

We may therefore go on to consider the actual pieces of evidence in so far as they are relevant to our question.

I. Aristotle, *De Anima* A 2, 405 a 29: παραπλησίως δὲ τούτοις καὶ Ἀλκμαίων ἔοικεν ὑπολαβεῖν περὶ ψυχῆς. φησὶ γὰρ αὐτὴν ἀθάνατον εἶναι διὰ τὸ ἐοικέναι τοῖς ἀθανάτοις, τοῦτο δ' ὑπάρχειν αὐτῇ ὡς ἀεὶ κινουμένῃ. κινεῖσθαι γὰρ τὰ θεῖα πάντα συνεχῶς ἀεί, σελήνην, ἥλιον, τοὺς ἀστέρας καὶ τὸν οὐρανὸν ὅλον.

II. Diogenes Laërtius, VIII 83: καὶ τὴν σελήνην καθόλου ⟨τε τὰ ὑπὲρ⟩[1] ταύτην ἔχειν ἀίδιον φύσιν...ἔφη δὲ καὶ τὴν ψυχὴν ἀθάνατον καὶ κινεῖσθαι αὐτὴν συνεχὲς ὡς τὸν ἥλιον.

III. Aëtius, *Placita* II 16, 2, 3: Ἀλκμαίων καὶ οἱ μαθηματικοὶ τοὺς πλανήτας τοῖς ἁπλανέσιν ἀπὸ δυσμῶν ἐπ' ἀνατολὰς ἀντιφέρεσθαι.

IV. Stobaeus, *Eclogae Physicae* I 25, ex Aëtio: Ἀλκμαίων πλατὺν εἶναι τὸν ἥλιον. *Id. ib.* I 26: Ἀλκμαίων Ἡράκλειτος Ἀντιφῶν κατὰ

---

[1] add. Diels. καὶ ὅλον τὸν οὐρανόν Zeller.

τὴν τοῦ σκαφοειδοῦς στροφὴν καὶ τὰς περικλίσεις [σελήνης ἔκλειψιν γενέσθαι].

V. Aristotle, *Problemata* XVII 3, 916a 33: τοὺς ἀνθρώπους φησὶν ὁ ᾿Αλκμαίων διὰ τοῦτο ἀπόλλυσθαι ὅτι οὐ δύνανται τὴν ἀρχὴν τῷ τέλει προσάψαι, κομψῶς εἰρηκὼς εἴ τις ὡς τύπῳ φράζοντος αὐτοῦ ἀποδέχοιτο καὶ μὴ διακριβοῦν ἐθέλει τὸ λεχθέν.

VI. Theophrastus, *De Sensu* 25: τῶν δὲ μὴ τῷ ὁμοίῳ ποιούντων τὴν αἴσθησιν ᾿Αλκμαίων μὲν πρῶτον ἀφορίζει τὴν πρὸς τὰ ζῷα διαφοράν. ἄνθρωπον γάρ φησι τῶν ἄλλων διαφέρειν ὅτι μόνον ξυνίησι, τὰ δὲ ἄλλα αἰσθάνεται μέν, οὐ ξυνίησι δέ, ὡς ἕτερον ὂν τὸ φρονεῖν καὶ αἰσθάνεσθαι καὶ οὐ, καθάπερ ᾿Εμπεδοκλῆς, ταὐτόν. *Id. ib.* 26: ἁπάσας δὲ τὰς αἰσθήσεις συνηρτῆσθαί πως πρὸς τὸν ἐγκέφαλον.

Of these passages, we may take the first four together because of their concern with the οὐρανός. The fourth need not detain us. We may gather from it that Alcmaeon's interest was not in astronomical details but in the laws governing the orderly motions of the heavens. We should not, however, assume with Burnet that Alcmaeon's views on the sun and on eclipses were "so crude" that he can hardly have "invented" the doctrine of the contrary motions of οὐρανός and planets. He did not invent, but he probably did accept this doctrine. We notice that the *Placita* attribute it to ᾿Αλκμαίων καὶ οἱ μαθηματικοί, implying that Alcmaeon stood apart but still held the doctrine that the learned members of the Brotherhood later elaborated.

We may distinguish two stages in this elaboration, not implying thereby any rigid distinction in time—though the first must have been the earlier. First there is the purely astronomical interest. We can only reconstruct Anaximander's οὐρανός conjecturally, but if we combine Burnet's explanation of the ἄπειροι οὐρανοί with Cornford's suggestion that ἄπειρον implies the rounded sphere— and, however it may be in the case of ultimate "space", the γόνιμον which was "separated out through the eternal motion" was probably ἄπειρον in this sense—we arrive at a primitive form of the later geocentric astronomy—three planetary bands and a containing sphere of stars.[1] But there is no evidence of a daily rotation of this οὐρανός,

[1] Burnet, *E. G. Ph.*[4] p. 69. (I do not of course accept the δῖνος theory there stated.) Cornford, "The Invention of Space", in *Essays in Honour of Gilbert Murray*, 1936.

though the rotation of the earth, which Burnet would find in Anaximander, is less likely than such a rotation. In Anaximenes, if we may trust the tradition recorded in Aëtius,[1] we find the stars "nailed to the crystal sphere, though some say they are (or if Heath's emendation is right, "while some of them are") fiery leaves, like pictures". This may explain the "flat" sun of Alcmaeon, and it is clear that Anaximenes recognised planetary motions, though it is not clear that he recognised the motion of the crystalline sphere as a whole. If we may suppose that Pythagoras knew of these Milesian adumbrations of a doctrine of the οὐρανός and of contrary motions of stars and planets, it is no longer unreasonable to suppose him responsible for giving it clear and definite form as an astronomical scheme. This scheme is of such historic importance that its immediate significance for the earliest Pythagoreans is easily forgotten. Burnet,[2] for instance, is so concerned to deny that anyone conceived of planetary spheres before Eudoxus[3] that he almost ignores the importance of the recognition by Pythagoras—if not by Anaximenes—of the solid containing sphere of the fixed stars, which henceforth sets the limit for all the cosmic motions and by its rotation marks the period of day and night. This is far more important than the recognition of the planetary motions in the contrary sense, which it necessitated.

For this spherical οὐρανός, accepted first from the astronomers, must have given the early Pythagoreans much matter for thought. Here it is that the second stage in the development of the doctrine begins. It involves a turning away from the physical fact to the mathematical law and the geometric figure. We leave the naturalism that is the mark of the Ionian succession. For the Milesians, though the stars were "gods" in a sense—they were the most notable

---

[1] Aëtius II 14, 3 (Diels, *F. d. V.*[5] 13 A 14); Heath, *Aristarchus*, pp. 42 sqq.

[2] *E. G. Ph.*[3] p. 110; *ib.* § 93.

[3] Adam was no doubt wrong in following Zeller's opinion that planetary spheres are implied in the myth of Er (*ad Rep.* x 616b sqq.). Even if they were, it would not signify, for the myth is not intended to dogmatise on astronomical matters. In the *Timaeus* there are only "paths" of the planets, not "solid" cart-wheels, still less are the orbits of the several fixed stars "solid": the outer sphere is not necessarily more "solid" than what it contains (*v.* Cornford, *Plato's Cosmology*, p. 119).

aggregates of life-stuff—yet the philosophic interest was rather in their physical constitutions. Anaximander's γόνιμον breaking out into rings of flame and Anaximenes's stars which were like leaves or like studs on the crystalline sphere are the precursors of the impious astronomy of Anaxagoras and the open materialism of the Atomists. The Pythagoreans approached the question from the other side. They looked for the rational mathematical law, observing as they did so the logical perfection of the spherical form.[1] When Plato in the *Timaeus* makes those who looked into the heavens but no farther turn into birds in the next life[2] he is speaking in the true Pythagorean tradition.

But we are concerned with two thinkers in this early Pythagorean period, neither of whom was orthodox. Parmenides went further than Pythagoras in concerning himself with the ontological and epistemological instead of the mathematical, but these very considerations encouraged him to declare Being a "well-rounded sphere",[3] albeit motionless. We cannot concern ourselves with the problems of the two parts of his system, or even with detailed interpretation of the first part. Without in any way committing ourselves to a "materialistic" interpretation of the One Being, we are able to recognise that the astronomical doctrine of the spherical οὐρανός, worked upon by a generation of μαθηματικοί, must lie behind Parmenides, so that his system is far less intelligible without it. It was, after all, the reverse process, the recognition of the οὐρανός as revealing the perfection of the sphere, which made the fusion between ontology, astronomy, and epistemology possible for Plato in the *Timaeus*. The "signs" of the One Being (other than ἀκίνητον) were acknowledged by Plato to belong to the soul of the οὐρανός no less than to the Forms, in so far as it could be considered to exhibit in its own life the perfect rationality of the rotating sphere.

But this insight could only be achieved when it had also been

---

[1] Ar. *De Caelo* B 4, 286 b, 10 sqq. (cf. *Probl.* XVI 10) seems to reflect such early Pythagorean thinking. Cf. also Diels's note on Parmenides fr. 3, 1 in *Parmenides Lehrgedicht*.

[2] *Tim.* 91 d 6 sqq.

[3] Cf. αὐτὰρ ἐπεὶ πεῖρας πύματον...οἱ γὰρ πάντοθεν ἶσον ὁμῶς ἐν πείρασι κύρει, fr. 8 (Diels), 42 sqq.

recognised that ἀκίνητον was not, after all, a sign of perfect reality; and to recognise this meant falling back on the older tradition of the earlier unorthodox Pythagorean, Alcmaeon. For him the soul was immortal because it resembled the heavenly bodies and the οὐρανός as a whole in its continuous motion. How far did Alcmaeon intend the analogy to be pressed? The danger for us is in caution rather than in extravagance, for what we call an analogy would be for Alcmaeon an actual resemblance. No doubt it is impossible to say exactly where Alcmaeon's ideas end and Plato's development of them begins, but the direct connection is evident, and we can best bring this out by contrasting other current conceptions that Plato evidently neglected because Alcmaeon's thinking provided him with the links he needed between empirical psychology and astronomy, between the human soul and the soul of the world.

We have already seen that the first axiom of the *Phaedrus* proof of the immortality of the soul had been formulated by Alcmaeon, namely that the ever-moving is the immortal. Alcmaeon would not see the necessity of postulating an everlasting self-moved source of motion, but he did seek to prove the immortality of the soul from the unquestioned immortality of the stars on the ground (not logically adequate, of course) of their common characteristic of τὸ ἀεὶ κινεῖσθαι. But we have to ask whether this συνεχὴς κίνησις means κυκλοφορία or not; for only if it does, can we regard Alcmaeon as a direct precursor of the *Timaeus*. A strong probability is all we can establish, but this it does seem possible to establish if we consider the inadequacy of other possible interpretations.

One might suppose that a quite indeterminate motion was intended, a kind of flow or permeation of life-stuff, like the motion native to the ἀρχή of the Ionians, or the mobile fire of the medical treatises that show Heraclitean affinities. But if we compare what we are told of Alcmaeon's views with such a fragment as the fifth of Diogenes of Apollonia, which is concerned with νόησις in his system,[1] we see how much nearer Alcmaeon is to the *Timaeus*. The Air controls and directs all creatures, and, though it varies in slight gradations throughout their kinds, is τὸ τὴν νόησιν ἔχον, wherever

[1] fr. 5 (Diels).

it is found. But the ξύνεσις, which according to Alcmaeon sets man apart from all the creatures and which the *Timaeus* would place only in the dominant part of soul in the head of man, cannot be compared in its nature or its motion with this all-pervading Air of Diogenes. Moreover, in his astronomy Diogenes followed Anaxagoras with a few emendations.[1] This implies at the least that he did not hold that the heavenly bodies are distinctively alive, for the parallel which he seems to imply between the air which animals breathe and the air "by the sun"[2] is hardly as clear as the analogy of macrocosm and microcosm in Anaximenes, and is quite insufficient evidence for a distinctive immortality either of man or of the stars. It is noticeable that the dogma of the divinity of the stars is absent from philosophical treatises between Alcmaeon and Plato.[3] The account of Pythagorean doctrine which is reported from Alexander Polyhistor at Diogenes Laertius VIII 25 is referred by Wellmann to a fourth-century Pythagorean, but he allows that it derives in part from Alcmaeon as well as from Plato and Aristotle.[4] At the very least we must assert that Alcmaeon added to the Milesian "ageless and deathless" as applied to the stars the sense that these "divine things" exhibited a continuous orderly movement. To attribute to him an Aristotelian distinction of sublunary and celestial[5] is, of course, a mere blunder; but it may cover the recognition that stars and soul alike were composed of a distinctive fine substance, suited to their function and nature.

[1] Burnet, *E. G. Ph.*[4] pp. 356 sqq.

[2] fr. 5 (Diels). παρὰ τῷ ἡλίῳ seems to mean "in the vicinity of the sun", not air within the sun which is its "soul" (like the hotter air within living creatures). Burnet seems to base his statement that "the circular motion of the world is due to the intelligence of the Air" (*op. cit.* p. 357) on the solitary mention of τὴν ἐκ τοῦ θερμοῦ περιφορὰν in the short notice in Diogenes Laertius (IX 57). Even if valid, this is a cosmogonic motion like the περιχώρησις of Anaxagoras rather than regular circular motion of the heavenly bodies and the οὐρανός.

[3] Of course the doctrine remained in popular belief, Aristoph. *Pax* 832 sqq. Socrates prayed to the Sun after his vigil, Alcibiades tells us, *Symposium* 220 d.

[4] Especially D.L. VIII 27, 28 (Diels, *F. d. V.*[5] 58 B, 1a) and Wellmann, art. "Eine pythagoreische Urkunde" (*Hermes*, LIV, pp. 231 sqq.).

[5] Passage II *supr.*

If, then, this orderly movement was the special characteristic of the heavenly bodies, it would be this rather than a permeation or agitation that was also the special characteristic of the soul for Alcmaeon. It is true that some Pythagoreans taught, according to Aristotle, that the soul is "the motes in the air or that which moves them".[1] Though the affinities with Democritus, who also used the figure of the motes, suggest that this is a later doctrine akin to Pythagorean atomism, the phrase κἂν ᾖ νηνεμία παντελὴς in Aristotle may refer to a more primitive background[2]—though not necessarily. But even if it does, there seems no reason to suppose that Alcmaeon attributed such a motion to the soul, for there is no analogous astronomical phenomenon which could be said to exhibit such a motion. The twinkling of the stars receives no scientific notice before Aristotle so far as we know, and "the sun, the moon and the other planets", to whose motion the soul's motion is expressly compared, do not twinkle.[3]

We seem shut up to the explanation that Alcmaeon held that the orderly motions of the heavenly bodies, involving, presumably, the contrary movements of planets and fixed stars, were somehow reflected in the συνεχὴς κίνησις which guaranteed the immortality of the human soul. Seemingly in contradiction to this we have the saying that "man dies because he cannot join the beginning to the end" quoted as coming from Alcmaeon in the Aristotelian *Problems*,[4] and reappearing only in the paroemiographer Michael Apostolius.[5] He adds the simple explanation κύκλος γὰρ ἂν ἦν: the writer of the *Problem*, however, adds the interesting warning κομψῶς εἰρηκὼς εἴ τις ὡς τύπῳ φράζοντος αὐτοῦ ἀποδέχοιτο, καὶ μὴ διακριβοῦν ἐθέλει τὸ λεχθέν. It is perhaps worth while to disregard his warning or

---

[1] *De Anima* A 2, 404a 16 sqq.

[2] Cf. *Phaedo* 77d 5 sqq.; Rohde, *Psyche*, Eng. tr. ch. XIII, n. 115.

[3] *De Caelo* B 8, 290a 18 sqq. Rohde (*op. cit.* ch. XI, nn. 35, 40) tries to explain the motion of the soul in Alcmaeon along these lines, but fails to explain in what sense the motions of τὰ θεῖα, "moon, sun, stars and heaven", resemble the motes in a sunbeam! ἀστήρ and ἄστρον often mean "planet" in Aristotle without further qualification.

[4] Passage V *supr.*

[5] *Corpus paroemiographorum* (ed. Leutsch et Schneidewein), II 674.

rather to look for the reasons for it. Following, it may be, the lost work of Aristotle Πρὸς τὰ ᾽Αλκμαίωνος, he is quite possibly discounting an interpretation of the saying which takes it, along with the other fragments concerning the soul, as meaning that the circles of the stars in their courses are always completed while those in the soul of man fail. Aristotle would reject any idea of circles in the soul, as his explicit criticism of the *Timaeus* in the *De Anima* makes clear,[1] and so anything more specific than a general reference to the "period" of the year, for instance,[2] would be objectionable to him as an interpretation of Alcmaeon's saying: the precisians' version may nevertheless have been correct.

We have direct evidence of the importance Alcmaeon gave to the brain as the seat of ξύνεσις. We cannot be certain how much of the account of cognition which Aristotle seems to have taken over in the *Posterior Analytics* from a passage in the *Phaedo* is to be traced to Alcmaeon,[3] but we can be sure that he regarded ξύνεσις as capable of dealing with the data of the sense-organs.[4] Aetius, speaking in Stoic terms, says he placed τὸ ἡγεμονικόν in the brain.[5] The brain can only receive the reports of the sense-organs if it is unimpaired,[6] but it is the brain which "furnishes the sensations". This teaching must have been related to the ἰσονομία doctrine. The seed was

[1] *De Anima* A 3, 406b 26 sqq.
[2] Even less likely is an interpretation based on the doctrine of Ar. *De Gen. et Corr.* B 10, 336b sqq. that γεννητὰ καὶ φθαρτά and ἁπλᾶ σώματα imitate κυκλοφορητά as far as possible. The racial succession and reciprocal transformation are here regarded as circles; by means of them men *do* join the beginning to the end. The general reference to a period or cycle of life cannot be disregarded altogether, but there must be some more specific reference. Signorella Luigia Stella (*op. cit.* p. 273 *fin.*; *v. supr.* p. 36, n. 1) accepts a mystical mathematical interpretation although admitting it to be inconsistent with Alcmaeon's naturalism which she has contrasted with the Pythagorean and Orphic attitudes elsewhere (*ib.* pp. 255, 265).
[3] *Anal. Post.* II 19; cf. also *Phys.* VII 247b with *Phaedo* 96b 4.
[4] Theophrastus seems uncertain how the senses were related to the brain (πως, passage VI *supr.*), but his classing of Alcmaeon with those who make perception μὴ τῷ ὁμοίῳ suggests that he thought Alcmaeon held that sense-data are dealt with by ξύνεσις, a faculty of a different order.
[5] fr. 17 (Wachtler); Plut. *Epit.* V 17, 3 (Diels, *D.G.* 427a 8).
[6] fr. 8 (Wachtler); Theophr. *De Sensu*, 26 *fin.*

a portion of the brain,[1] and the brain was formed first in the embryo;[2] therefore, presumably, it exercised a directing force on the pairs of opposite δυνάμεις that composed the body and imposed ἰσονομία upon them. All this taken together does not bring us the whole way to the controlling circles in the human head, which we find in the *Timaeus*;[3] but it at least suggests how such an idea can have seemed to have "scientific" backing: moreover, if Alcmaeon's astronomical ideas and the saying about man's failure to join beginning to end belong to the same περὶ φύσεως as the more empirical teaching about the brain, there was all the material for a bridge to be built between astronomy and psychology even if the bridge itself was not yet there.

The superficial contradiction between the saying that man dies and the statement that the soul is immortal because it resembles the stars is easily resolved if Alcmaeon believed in transmigration; but there is no evidence that he did, and his radical distinction between man and the beasts suggests that he did not. Here the *Timaeus* seems to reveal a difficult accommodation of opposing views. Transmigration and the tripartite soul seem Pythagorean additions to a simpler original scheme in which the soul of man is located entirely

[1] Aëtius v 3, 3; Diels, *D.G.* 417.
[2] Aëtius v 17, 3. Plato gives embryology the most cursory treatment of all the sciences, at *Tim.* 91 c, d.
[3] The passage in περὶ ἱερῆς νούσου xix, where the brain is called τῶν ἀπὸ τοῦ ἠέρος γιγνομένων ἑρμηνεύς and ἐς τὴν ξύνεσιν διαγγέλλων, seems at first very close to Alcmaeon, especially if Alcmaeon's account of smell reported by Theophrastus (Diels, *D.G.* 506, 25) and Aetius iv 171 is misunderstood to mean that the air inhaled is to be identified with ξύνεσις (for it only stimulates the action of ξύνεσις by reporting to it). On περὶ ἱερῆς νούσου xix, xx one may refer to a note by Dr W. H. S. Jones in the Loeb Hippocrates (postscript to vol. i): "The brain is regarded by the writer as a filter of the air, keeping its quintessence; thus the brain, though in some sense the seat of *sensus communis*, is nevertheless also a passive instrument of the universal consciousness." We remember how Socrates distinguishes between the theory that we think with air (or water or fire), which is this writer's theory, and the theory that "it is none of these things, but it is the brain itself which gives rise to sense experiences". (*Phaedo*, 96 b.) Hirzel (*Hermes*, xi, p. 240) pointed out that this refers to Alcmaeon. He alone really anticipates the *Timaeus*.

in the head, the body being a mere "carriage" for it.[1] In the head, or rather in the brain, is a replica of the planetary system, a set of circles which preserve and maintain rational life as long as they run true.[2] When the forces from outside break into this vessel of the soul so as to inhibit these circles irremediably, man dies;[3] but the soul retires to its kind, which always functions in the heavens, until it is associated again with some other orrery in another infant's head.

This is the simple scheme, fantastic as it sounds to us, which Plato seems to have derived from Alcmaeon, perhaps with his own elaboration. But the transmigration doctrine and the need of a universal biology required him to take the souls of all living creatures into account and a tripartite human soul had to be located within the human body.[4] This led to the strange extravagance concerning the origin of the various shapes of the heads of the beasts, whose "heads were drawn down to earth by natural affinity and rested there, and their skulls grew elongated and of various shapes, according to the deformations produced in their several circles by inactivity".[5]

[1] *Tim.* 44 d; cf. *ib.* 34 e.
[2] In the infant the "circle of the Same" in the soul is stopped but cannot be broken (*v.* 44 d, e). The circle of the Different is twisted out of shape.
[3] *Tim.* 81 d, e (senile decay), 85 e (disease).
[4] The disparity between Alcmaeonic and Pythagorean trends in the *Timaeus* is similar to the tension between the tripartition and the simplicity of the soul in *Rep.* x 611 b (*v.* Adam *ad loc.*, Jackson, *J. Phil.* x, pp. 120 sqq.). We are not told explicitly that the soul moves in circles in the seats of the two θνητὰ εἴδη ψυχῆς. (Cf. 70 a, 70 e, 87 a and especially 90 a–d, where the κινήσεις are prescribed as necessary for all three parts of the soul, but only in the case of the highest part in the head is there mention of περίοδοι.)
[5] 91 e *fin.* This ingenuity is foreign to Alcmaeon with his radical distinction between men and beasts, but might be a *tour de force* of one desiring to accommodate his ideas to Pythagoreanism. We cannot even be sure that Alcmaeon held that the brain was spherical in shape. The discussion on the sutures in the Hippocratic *Wounds in the Head* to which Taylor appeals (*Comm.* pp. 536, 537 on *Tim.* 76 a 6–b 1) seems strictly relevant to the matter of the treatise and it can only be conjecture to trace it back to Alcmaeon—though the observable fact of the imperfect joining of the sutures in the infant's head fits in admirably with the *Timaeus* account.

The one constant factor throughout the dialogue, from the first account of the planting of the soul in the infant's ἐπίρρυτον καὶ ἀπόρρυτον σῶμα to this last descent to four-footed beasts, lizards and shellfish, is the insistence throughout on the presence of the soul-circles. We are told in general terms at 44a of τὸ τῆς ψυχῆς ἅπαν κύτος, and this is elaborated in the later physiological section of the dialogue. The head is there called the ἀγγεῖον: it contains the spherical brain, the "ploughland that is to contain the divine seed"; this is protected within the marrow and the marrow within the spinal column as within a stone fence:[1] only when disease or old age causes this to yield to the onslaughts of the outer triangles does death ensue. Life depends on the existence, and a good life on the freeing from encumbrances and distortion, of this inner solar system, which may function in each region of the soul[2]—this is obscure—but does so supremely in the head.

This inner system, which can be overthrown only by the undermining of the guardian marrow, is quite distinct from the circulatory,

[1] λιθοειδεῖ περιβόλῳ συνέφραξεν, 74a. The whole account of the formation of the marrow is told in detail befitting its importance (73b sqq.). Note especially that the brain is its *spherical* termination.

[2] The reference to στρογγύλα καὶ προμήκη σχήματα (73d) which compose the vessels of the "mortal element of soul" is, of course, a reference to the marrow in the vertebrae of the spinal column. Whether the soul within imitated the formation without we cannot say (cf. p. 48 *supr.* n. 5). The question arises again when we come to the account of the actual bone of the vertebrae at 74a. Here Taylor's explanation of the phrase τῇ θατέρου προσχρώμενος δυνάμει is not very satisfactory, and Cornford's return to Fraccaroli seems right (Taylor, *Comm.* p. 527; Cornford, *Plato's Cosmology*, p. 295 *init.*: see the whole discussion, *ib.* pp. 293–296). But Cornford has already interpreted 73d as meaning that the vertebrae are no more than anchor-chains binding the two lower components of the soul to the head. It seems more likely that ἡ τοῦ θατέρου δύναμις is considered to "circulate" through the whole spinal marrow other than the brain. But the point remains obscure. Cf. 72d: τὰ μὲν οὖν περὶ ψυχῆς, ὅσον θνητὸν ἔχει καὶ ὅσον θεῖον, καὶ ὅπη, καὶ μεθ' ὧν, καὶ δι' ἃ χωρὶς ᾠκίσθη, τὸ μὲν ἀληθές, ὡς εἴρηται, θεοῦ ξυμφήσαντος τότ' ἂν οὕτω διισχυριζοίμεθα. We note that the immaterial ψυχή has the μυελός as its immediate κύτος, while the skull and vertebrae are the ἀγγεῖον of both; but there is no question of the μυελός serving as a kind of "pineal gland": the marrow must be kept apart from the fluxes of the body and the bone is there simply for protection.

digestive and respiratory system which serves to maintain the body and the marrow itself. This differentiates the *Timaeus* from all the medical treatises, including even the first book of the περὶ διαίτης. Here Dr Peck[1] sees close similarity to the *Timaeus* which may arise from common obligations to such a writer as Philistion. So long as the parallel is confined to the respiratory and digestive system in the *Timaeus*, it is no doubt valid; but it fails at once if we attempt to equate the account of the περὶ διαίτης with the "circles of the soul". Plato distinguishes absolutely between the περίωσις[2] of the respiratory and digestive processes and the περίοδοι of the soul, while the περὶ διαίτης, though it certainly distinguishes between soul and body, regards both as a blend of fire and water. The circuits there are circuits in the body[3] and akin to the περίωσις of the *Timaeus* rather than to its περίοδοι.

What then are we to make of this unique system of circles in the soul, and particularly in the head? When Plato wrote the *Cratylus*, he could make fun of the philosophers who "projected" the whirl in their own heads upon the innocent universe.[4] We see only too

---

[1] In his unpublished treatise *Pseudo-Hippocrates Philosophus*, which he very generously allowed me to inspect. The περὶ διαίτης contains remarkable passages in which an astronomical analogy is developed (especially ch. LXXXIX in the fourth book on which Dr Jones comments in his Loeb edition, Intro. p. lii). But whatever the astronomy implied there is no parallel between this analogy between stars and bodily circuits and Alcmaeon's analogy between the heavenly bodies and the soul.

[2] It is true that Plato himself draws an analogy between περίωσις and περίοδοι when he tells us (at 81 b 1) that the contents of the blood imitate the motions of the οὐρανός like the σφίγγειν exerted by its περίοδοι (at 58a sqq.). But this does not imply that the περίωσις is caused by νοῦς in the same sense as the movement of the οὐρανός is so caused. Plato is really thinking only of similar effects of the law of "like to like" in the universe and in the digestive system: if the οὐρανός analogy were pressed, the bodily frame would have to rotate as a whole, and this even Plato does not suggest.

[3] Cf. ch. XIX (tr. Jones): "Basket-makers turn their baskets round as they plait them; they end at the place from which they begin. The circuit in the body is the same; it ends where it begins." Cf. also ch. IV, l. 18 (Jones): ἑκάστη δὲ ψυχή... περιφοιτᾷ τὰ μόρια τὰ ἑωυτῆς. This implies a "progress" through the body, quite alien to Alcmaeon and Plato.

[4] *Crat.* 411 b.

clearly how the laugh can be turned against him in these sections of the *Timaeus*. He would, of course, reply that the περιχωρήσεις of Anaxagoras and his followers were arbitrary and mechanical while his were the direct evidence of νοῦς. There may be some humour intended in the explanation that man's head has a body lest it get irredeemably bunkered and that the heads of animals are less round in proportion as they are less intellectual, but Cornford's warning that Plato is probably serious in the main is a very necessary one.[1] Certainly his persistence in the conception of soul-circles through all difficulties is no *jeu d'esprit* nor is it a gentle caricature of a fifth-century Sicilian. The account of circulation, digestion and respiration and the pathology are combined, as Taylor points out, from several sources.[2] Some of these would be contemporary or recent, and yet they are all made to subserve this old doctrine of soul-circles harking back to Alcmaeon. The only explanation possible is that certain *a priori* requirements of Plato's thought were satisfied by this doctrine and by this doctrine alone and that therefore Plato held to it and bent everything else into subservience to it. This is a thing no fifth-century Pythagorean could have done or would have wished to do. Plato did it, and we have to discover why.

[1] Cornford, *Plato's Cosmology*, p. 151. Contrast Taylor, *Comm.* pp. 275, 642. There may be reference to Empedocles in the *Timaeus* passage as Taylor suggests, but on the whole the serious interpretation seems more likely; and Aristotle's "serious" treatment of the passage about animals' heads of which Taylor complains (Ar. *De Part. An.* 686a 27 sqq.) may not be as stupid as he would like to make out.

[2] *Comm.* pp. 587, 592, 600, 603, 607 sqq.

CHAPTER IV

ANTECEDENTS OF THE ΚΙΝΗΣΙΣ-DOCTRINE OF THE *TIMAEUS* IN THE SYSTEM OF EMPEDOCLES

The antecedents of Empedocles have generally been regarded as Orphism, Pythagoreanism and Parmenides. Otto Kern has pointed out, however, how little there is in him that is definitely Pythagorean,[1] and his debt to Parmenides and recognition of his doctrine, though definite, is but a small element in his poem.[2] Essentially Empedocles, like Xenophanes, teaches an enlightened and modified form of Orphism, though Xenophanes is far more drastic in his treatment of his traditional background, and gives us no cosmogony at all. But the εἷς θεός of Xenophanes, the σφαῖρος of Empedocles, the γόνιμον of Anaximander, and the earliest forms of the Pythagorean doctrine that later became the central-fire astronomy have all a common ancestor in the world-egg of the Orphics.[3] Alongside the more astronomical and mathematical doctrine of the οὐρανός, with the contrary motions of planets and fixed stars, there persisted the "ancient tale" which regarded the universe as a divine creature

---

[1] Otto Kern, "Empedokles und die Orphiker", *Archiv für Gesch. der Phil.* I (1888), pp. 498 sqq. Kern gives quotations to show that the lines of Empedocles on transmigration, which had been regarded as a distinctively Pythagorean trait in him, are almost verbal reproductions of Orphic verses (cf. frs. 222, 223 Abel with Empedocles frs. 115, 117).

[2] fr. 17 (Diels) 14–35 is really the only direct reference to Parmenides, important though it is, and this is rather an imitative retort to Parmenides. The lines beginning σὺ δ' ἄκουε λόγου στόλον οὐκ ἀπατηλόν (*ib.* l. 26) claim for the moving powers and the elements the completeness of self-sufficient being Parmenides had claimed for τὸ ὄν, and in the same terms. It is not, Empedocles affirms, an ἀπατηλὸς λόγος.

[3] This seems to be the explanation of the "embryological analogies" which Mr H. C. Baldry (*Class. Quart.* vol. XXVI) finds in Anaximander, the early "central-fire" and the ὑμήν of Leucippus (D.L. IX 31 sqq.). How far these thinkers used observed embryological data to regulate their use of the myth is not easy to determine: at any rate they never regarded it as "myth".

with a spherical body; and we cannot ignore the importance of this tradition for the *Timaeus*.

One cannot maintain, however, that the transmission of this Orphic cosmogonic tradition to the *Timaeus* came through Empedocles alone. After the passage explaining that the body of the universe must contain fire to be visible and earth to be tangible, and that its three dimensions demand two "mean" substances, we revert to an archaic passage explaining the need for the sphericity of the οὐρανός. The first sentences of this explanation are not archaic at all, however: they give the kind of reasoning that we have previously suggested went on among the first generation of Pythagoreans concerning the perfection of the sphere:[1]

For its figure he gave it that which was fitting and in keeping with its nature. Now, for the living creature which was to embrace all living creatures the fitting figure must be that which contains all figures in itself. Therefore he wrought it on his lathe spherical and round, with centre equidistant from extremity in every direction, the figure of all others most perfect and uniform, judging regularity beyond compare more perfect than irregularity.

But we go on from this to an explanation why the Demiurge made its outer surface smooth which takes us at once to a more primitive stratum of thinking:[2]

It had no need of eyes, for nothing was left outside it to be seen; nor yet of ears, for there was nothing to be heard; there was no air around it to call for respiration; nor again had it need of organs wherewith to take its nutriment into itself or excrete it once more when drained of its juices. Nothing was given off from it, nothing entered it—there was nothing but itself: it was contrived by art to feed on its own waste, to act wholly on itself and to be acted on by itself alone. For he that contrived it thought it would be better self-sufficient than dependent on anything else. He saw no need to give it superfluous hands, which it would require neither for grasping nor for defence, nor yet feet or other support to stand on.[3] For he had assigned it the motion proper to its body, that one of the seven which has most to do with understanding and intelligence. Accordingly he spun it uniformly upon itself in the same volume

[1] *Tim.* 33b, tr. Taylor.   [2] *Ib.* 33c.
[3] Contrast the needs of the human head mentioned at 44d, e.

and made it revolve in a circle; the other six motions he denied it, giving it no part in their aberrations. And since feet were not wanted for this revolution, he begat it without feet or legs.

The conception of the world as a living creature that we have in this passage seems to be precisely the conception against which Xenophanes protested and of which his εἷς θεός is a refinement. But Xenophanes made a far more radical protest against its anthropomorphism: his One God is "like unto mortals neither in bodily form nor in mind". Plato's Demiurge seems to do little more than lop off the needless excrescences of an anthropomorphic world-god in order to smooth his outer surface. We are reminded of the spherical, bi- sexual creatures in Aristophanes's speech in the *Symposium*,[1] who sped about like the acrobats on their two pairs of legs. They too were smoothed down on their "outer" side when they were cut in half and had their organs transferred to the "inner" side, and cutting them was like splitting sorb-apples or *eggs* with hairs.[2] The Ouranos stays where it is and needs no legs for its revolutions. What is later described in the account of mutual transformations of the various bodies is here described anthropomorphically as the consuming of its own waste by the Ouranos.

In this passage we see Plato taking as much of the old Orphic material as suits his purpose. He is concerned to retain the feeling that the universe is a divine creature, while making its sphericity "exact" and insisting that it is both self-sufficient and self-contained—

[1] *Symposium* 189e sqq. A valuable examination of the original Orphic verses, the *Symposium*, Empedocles and Anaximander was made by Konrat Ziegler in an article "Menschen- und Weltenwerden" (*Neue Jahrbücher für das klass. Alt.* XXXI (1913), pp. 529 sqq.). His view of the relations of Orphic cosmogony, Empedocles and Aristophanes in the *Symposium* is indicated in his diagram (*ib.* p. 570):

Orphische Anthropogonie

Empedokles

Kontamination

Platon-Aristophanes

[2] *Symp.* 190d. Bury *ad loc.* thinks of Orphic magic: there is also the reference to the World-egg, and this is obviously spherical. (I now think that ὅα is the correct reading at *Symposium* 190 d.)

that there is no surrounding void, as there is in the early forms of the "central-fire" doctrine[1] (Plato, like Xenophanes, denies that the world breathes), nor any internal void, but only the mutual transformation of its content.

There is nothing in all this that one can attribute directly to the influence of Empedocles, though Empedocles seems in his Sphairos to be making the same modifications of the primitive Orphism in respect to the universe as a whole. There can be little doubt that he regarded the universe as spherical: the evidence to the contrary is that he said it was "like an egg". But so was the Orphic world, which was spherical nevertheless, and if Empedocles had really held the view attributed to him by Stobaeus[2] that the height of the world was greater than its breadth, it is inconceivable that Aristotle would not have commented on its difficulties in the *De Caelo*, when discussing the possibility of the universe being lentiform or oviform. The tradition, however, is very significant in that it indicates how closely Empedocles kept to the Orphic cosmogony, and in this to the Rhapsodic theogony in particular. Parmenides would never have said that the world was "in the shape of the Egg".

---

[1] On this *v.* ch. v *infr.* p. 71.

[2] Stobaeus, *Ecl.* I 26 (Diels, *F. d. V.*⁵ 31 A 50; *D.G.* 363 b 5). Aristotle points out (*De Caelo* 287 a 20) that if the world were lentiform or oviform "we should have to admit space and void outside the moving body, because the whole body would not always occupy the same room". This would be true of the turnings of the "hemisphere of light", were Empedocles's world oviform in the technical sense, as Zeller says. The Stobaeus passage seems to imply confusion with an Epicurean tradition, which, allowing the general principle that a world could assume other shapes than the spherical, held that at one stage in its evolution it is oviform. (Diels, *D.G.* p. 329 a 5 sqq. (Plut. *Epit.* II 2, 3); *ib.* p. 589 (Epiphanius, *Adv. Haer.* 18).) The passages in which Empedocles follows Parmenides imply a sphere as the necessary shape of the universe, and Empedocles himself regards the σφαῖρος as κυκλοτερής. There is no evidence that the shape of the whole changed during the reign of Strife. On the contrary, the first effect of the entrance of νεῖκος to break up the σφαῖρος was for the air, hardened by the fire, to form a "crystalline sphere" (Diels, *D.G.* 33 D; *F. d. V.*⁵ 31 A 51, 52).

Ziegler's article, *Neue Jahrbücher*, XXXI, pp. 529 sqq., goes into the Orphic evidence in fullest detail, in explaining the origin of the *Kugelmenschen* in the *Symposium*. Cf. also Kern, *A.G.P.* I, p. 502.

But the real link between Empedocles and the *Timaeus* is, of course, with the later part of the dialogue, though not so much with the physiology as with the account of the motions and interfusion of the four bodies falsely called "elements". The criticism that "these are not even the syllables, let alone the alphabet"[1] of nature shows how drastically Empedocles is dealt with by Plato, although his ideas, and particularly those of the two causes of motion, Love and Strife, do lie behind what is written in the *Timaeus*. In the case of the στοιχεῖα, the further analysis into triangles probably puts Plato further ahead of Empedocles than Empedocles was of Onomacritus and the Orphic tradition,[2] but there is less need for modification of the moving causes. For with Plato, as with Empedocles, the four bodies have no "source of motion and rest" in themselves. The hylozoist φύσις and even the world-god of Xenophanes[3] had motion inherent in their nature. Parmenides by his denial of this inherent motion makes its assertion afterwards conscious and deliberate. Anaxagoras posits an outside factor to set up the περιχώρησις of his intermingled "real things", which, by themselves, would be as static as the One of Melissus. The Atomists boldly demand motion in the same way as they demand void, and Aristotle charges them with ῥᾳθυμία for this. Aristotle himself posits the ἁπλᾶ σώματα, but he goes back to the hylozoists in his view of the origin of their motion: his refinement on them is simply in his doctrine of tendency to natural places. All is not water, air, earth, or fire, but each of these exists and has its place and tends by its inherent motion to seek it. Plato, like Empedocles and Anaxagoras, insists that the motion of the bodies, four or many, is not of themselves but proceeds from separate moving causes of a psychic order. It is true that νοῦς is called λεπτότατον and that φιλία and νεῖκος are sometimes spoken of as though they are refined material forces,[4] but it is their

---

[1] *Tim.* 48 b *fin.* c *init.*   [2] Diels, *D.G.* p. 610.

[3] fr. 26 (Diels) αἰεὶ δ' ἐν ταὐτῷ μίμνει...κ.τ.λ....seems only to deny movement of the whole universe in absolute space: the divine life is motion in one sense and the changes of earth and water are physical motions.

[4] στοργὴν δὲ στοργῆι κ.τ.λ....(Diels, fr. 109) and such phrases as ἠπιόφρων Φιλότητος ἀμεμφέος ἄμβροτος ὁρμή (fr. 35, l. 13 Diels) are

tendency toward the immaterial and the clear differentiation of the moving powers from the ὁμοῦ πᾶν and from the four roots respectively which are the peculiar characteristics of the doctrine of the αἰτία κινήσεως in Anaxagoras and Empedocles.

Aristotle's criticisms of Empedocles which concern themselves with his doctrine of κίνησις[1] elaborate the charge that he makes both moving powers responsible for both mingling and separation: φιλία separates the homogeneous masses of each body to create the μεῖγμα, while νεῖκος congregates the masses out of the μεῖγμα each to its kind;[2] and this seems to contravene any identification of Friendship with goodness and Strife with evil. Elsewhere it is the conception of τύχη in the system that troubles Aristotle. If νεῖκος causes the αἰθήρ to rise, why say that "it ran together now so, then so, as it chanced",[3] with the other elements?[4]

This question of τύχη reminds us of a passage in the tenth book of the Laws where a reference to Empedocles has been found by commentators because of the apparent similarity of the doctrine there criticised to the doctrine of τύχη in Empedocles as stated and criticised by Aristotle in the second book of the Physics.[5] But Mr Tate[6] has recently shown that the reference in the Laws is more probably to fourth-century followers of Archelaus, who held a doctrine of sheer mechanical and fortuitous motion of the four bodies as "natural" and all else as due to art and chance. If this reference is true, there is all the more reason for thinking that Plato

the strongest evidence available from Empedocles himself for a quasi-material interpretation of the moving causes. Thus in fr. 17 l. 20 καὶ Φιλότης ἐν τοῖσιν ἴση μῆκός τε πλάτος τε is followed at once by τὴν σὺ νόῳ δέρκευ, μηδ' ὄμμασιν ἧσο τεθηπώς.

[1] Especially De Gen. et Corr. 315 a 3 sqq.; 333 b 30 sqq. Joachim's comments are at pp. 68, 69, 238, 239 of his edition.

[2] Ar. Metaph. A 4, 985 a 22 sqq.

[3] Emped. fr. 53; Phys. B 4, 196 a 21.   [4] So Diels takes συνέκυρσε.

[5] Laws x 889 a sqq.; Ar. Phys. B 8, 198 b 10 sqq.

[6] Class. Quart. xxx, pp. 48 sqq. I take a view diametrically opposed to that expressed by Professor Taylor (Comm. Intro. p. xix): "What Plato himself really thought about a good deal of Empedocles has to be learned not from our dialogue but from Laws x, where Empedocles more than anyone else is plainly aimed at in the exposure of the defects of 'naturalism'."

understood and used Empedocles's moving powers in the *Timaeus*, precisely because they did not require either unexplained mechanical motion of the bodies as did Archelaus and the Atomists, or motions naturally inherent in them as did the doctrine of Aristotle.

The conclusion to which we are pointed is a close relation of νεῖκος in Empedocles to ἀνάγκη in the *Timaeus*. We shall have to distinguish later on between all ξυναίτια and the two αἰτίαι, νοῦς and ἀνάγκη (or the πλανωμένη αἰτία).[1] Cornford's long discussion of ἀνάγκη[2] brings out the reason why such an αἰτία may be said to work τὸ τυχὸν καὶ ἄτακτον:[3] it is the antithesis of physical determinism. But Cornford sees in the account in the *Timaeus* a survival of yet another αἰτία κινήσεως, the old principle that "like seeks like", functioning over and above νοῦς and ἀνάγκη. This principle appears chiefly, according to him, in the account of the drifting together of the aggregates of various types of body due to the shaking of the Receptacle after the manner of the winnowing-basket. But this account of "what one would expect the world to be like when God is not there"[4] is not so far removed from the reign of Strife in the cycle of Empedocles. We must, of course, heed the warning Cornford gives: "Contrast Empedocles' four elements, which are all equal in quantity and evenly matched, so that they prevail in turn in the cycle of time. The determination of the four bodies in a geometrical proportion was a work of the Demiurge, which has not yet taken place."[5] But when this geometry of God has been removed or is not yet performed what is left is not ἀναίτιος, nor is it to be attributed merely to an unexplained tendency of like to seek like. This can only arise from the action of the πλανωμένη αἰτία. The phrase about the "shaking" of the ὑποδοχή is difficult: Apelt remarks on its apparent incompatibility with the conception of the ὑποδοχή as "mere space".[6] But the difficulty is only in the

---

[1] Ch. vi *infr.*
[2] *Plato's Cosmology*, pp. 161 sqq.; cf. *ib.* Epilogue, p. 361.
[3] *Tim.* 46e 5; Cornford, *op. cit.* p. 172.
[4] *Tim.* 53b; Cornford, *op. cit.* pp. 202, 203.
[5] Cornford, *op. cit.* p. 199 n. 2.
[6] *Tim.* 52e. Apelt, *Übers.* p. 171 n. 153: "Diese gewaltige Erschütterung verträgt sich schlecht mit dem Raume als solchem; aber ohne Unbegreiflichkeiten lassen sich Raum und Materie nicht identifizieren."

phrase: what is really meant is that the πλανωμένη αἰτία has command of all that is in the ὑποδοχή and sets up this form of motion. Plutarch[1] describes this πλανωμένη αἰτία as τὴν ἄτακτον καὶ ἀόριστον αὐτοκίνητον δὲ καὶ κινητικὴν ἀρχήν. Because Plutarch and Atticus took the passages of the *Timaeus* in which the disorderly pre-cosmic chaos is described as historical fact, we need not set aside their findings and interpretations simply because we agree, with Xenocrates, to regard the passages as an analysis. They are an analysis of what is going on, and the disorderly motions are a constant undercurrent in the actual cosmos. We have seen how Plato could adopt Empedocles to his purposes in the *Politicus* myth.[2] Now, when he comes to give a more exact account of his own cosmology, he abandons the idea of a cyclic world-process, but he uses the descriptions of the acosmic phase of that cycle to elucidate the constant acosmic element in his own cosmos. If ἀνάγκη could be identified with the ξύμφυτος ἐπιθυμία of the *Politicus* by Plutarch, all the more might he have identified it with the νεῖκος of Empedocles which lies behind the *Politicus* myth.

For ἀνάγκη, like νεῖκος in Empedocles, has for one of its effects this bringing of like to like, which Cornford would make into a separate moving force. Like νεῖκος, the working of ἀνάγκη makes against the interfusion of the four bodies and therefore an agency to counteract it must be sought. Plato shows no more enthusiasm than Empedocles for the tendency for each of the four bodies to drift off to its own place.[3] This is, for Empedocles and Plato alike, the acosmic tendency, not, as for Aristotle, the fulfilment of its destiny and the attainment of its form by the "simple body".[4] This cosmic "like to like" (which is a separation) is quite distinct from the theory of perception and nutrition of like by like—the latter being the only part that old principle plays in the system of Empedocles.

But if there is enough parallel between νεῖκος and ἀνάγκη for us to see direct influence of the former on the latter, is there any

---

[1] *De An. Procr. in Tim. Plat.* 1014e *init.*   [2] Cf. p. 26 *supr.*

[3] *Tim.* 57 c.

[4] Ar. *De Caelo*, Δ 3, 3 oa 33 sqq. Aristotle here says that this is "the real meaning" of the old principle of "like to like".

similar relation between φιλία and νοῦς? Here, of course, the position is very different. The whole development we have traced through Alcmaeon and Parmenides to the *Sophistes* and the *Philebus* must be taken into account, and the rotation which is the true εἰκών of the motions of νοῦς is a conception which is more advanced than anything in Empedocles, though certain phrases describing the Sphairos seem to be quite in keeping with it.[1] But there is no evidence that Empedocles went beyond the physical and meteorological descriptions of phenomena to find a rotation of the universe due to φιλία during the two periods of κόσμος in his cycle. We find hemispheres of light and darkness, which remind us rather of τὰ πρὸς δόξαν than of τὸ ὄν. The day was once nine months long, afterwards seven[2]—a thing quite as impossible for Plato as for Aristotle. Yet there is a place in the *Timaeus* at which we do seem to have a direct attribution to νοῦς of an effect like the effect of φιλία in the world of Empedocles. It arises out of the interaction between the rotation set up by νοῦς and the shaking apart of like to like by ἀνάγκη which we have just considered.

Empedocles seems to have believed in a containing sphere of air hardened by fire, at any rate during the two periods of κόσμος. This sphere set an arbitrary limit and confined the cosmic operations within itself. Plato's distinctive contribution in the *Timaeus* is to refuse an ἔσχατος κύκλος, and so to set himself radically against Eudoxus and Aristotle. It is true that in the earlier account of the body of the Ouranos incorporating the early Orphic ideas we are told of the "smoothness" and sphericity of the Ouranos before anything is said of its motion, as though it would be spherical however it moved; but even this does not imply a "containing" circumference materially distinct from the rest of the sphere. But later, when we make the

---

[1] Esp. fr. 28 (Diels): σφαῖρος κυκλοτερὴς μονίηι περιηγέι γαίων. μονίη is more probably related to μένειν than to μόνος. Whether περιηγής can imply motion is uncertain, but this is at least possible. Diels's "ringsum herrschende Einsamkeit" is not very convincing. The new L. and S. is inconsistent: the article on περιηγής follows Diels's interpretation but the article on μονίη takes it as derived from μένειν, quoting in support Diehl's reading at Tyrtaeus 1 15.

[2] Aëtius, *Plac.* v 18, 1 (Diels, *F. d. V.*⁵ 31 A 75).

new start[1] by bringing in the τρίτον γένος and study the motions of the πλανωμένη αἰτία, a more radical analysis is required. Plato's τιθήνη γενέσεως, which contains the unformed, shifting aggregates of the four bodies, cannot be regarded as spherical any more than its content can be regarded as "diaschematised". The sphericity of the Ouranos, no less than the basic triangles of the four bodies, is due to the demiurgic work of νοῦς. And the materials for the Demiurge are to be won over from the command of ἀνάγκη by "persuasion".

The movement set up by νοῦς is a physical κυκλοφορία and this seizes upon the four bodies which are already being moved by the separating movement of the πλανωμένη αἰτία. But the combined effect of these two movements would not give us the intermingling of the four bodies that we actually perceive: the difficulty arises which Plato states at 58a:[2]

But we have not explained how it is that the several bodies have not been completely separated apart in their kinds and so ceased to pass through one another and to change their place. We must then resume our explanation as follows. The circuit of the whole, when once it has comprehended the (four) kinds, being round and naturally tending to come together upon itself, constricts them all and allows (or tends to allow) no room to be left empty.[3] (ἡ τοῦ

---

[1] *Tim.* 47e sqq.　　　　　[2] Tr. Cornford, *op. cit.* p. 242.

[3] Archer Hind (*The Timaeus of Plato*, p. 209) found in this passage "a mighty inward pressure" which is "the second of Plato's two great dynamic powers". Cook Wilson did not attempt this particular throw, and it has been left to Taylor (*Comm.* pp. 397-399) to assert that σφίγγει means merely "clips round" and περίοδος merely "circuit"—circular form with no necessary implication of motion of any kind. Taylor claims Martin's support, who translates περίοδος "contour" and σφίγγει "reserre". (M. Rivaud, however, translates "Elle presse donc les uns contre les autres tous les éléments".) Cornford (*op. cit.* pp. 242-246) points out that so long as we banish Archer-Hind's arbitrary centripetal force there remains no reason to deny that περίοδος implies at once form and motion, since rotation and the spherical figure traced by it are for Plato inextricably associated (κυκλοτερὴς οὖσα καὶ πρὸς αὑτὴν πεφυκυῖα βούλεσθαι συνιέναι). Taylor's conception of "circular form" here is far from clear and his citation of the use of περίοδος for "the circuit of the walls" hardly elucidates it. To express *spherical* form, with no idea of motion, we should expect περιέχειν as we have it at *Tim.* 33b.

παντὸς περίοδος, ἐπειδὴ συμπεριέλαβεν τὰ γένη, κυκλοτερὴς οὖσα, καὶ πρὸς αὑτὴν πεφυκυῖα βούλεσθαι συνιέναι, σφίγγει πάντα καὶ κενὴν χώραν οὐδεμίαν ἐᾷ λείπεσθαι.)

This passage not only states a difficulty in the cosmological system but raises the question of the void and of the outer limit of the οὐρανός. The τιθήνη γενέσεως is called ἀνόρατον εἶδός τι καὶ ἄμορφον.[1] ἄμορφον refers in the first instance to the internal structure of the οὐρανός, the "forms" of the constituent triangles of the bodies, but it ought logically to hold good of the οὐρανός as a whole. There can be no compulsion for the οὐρανός to be spherical simply because space is spherical and because there is therefore no κενὴ χώρα that it could occupy. For Plato's χώρα is not an ἀγγεῖον. It does seem, however, that Plato never thought of the elements "drifting away to infinity"[2] as Taylor puts it: the void of Democritus is no more to be found here than the atoms. The reason seems to be partly that ἀνάγκη is a factor in an analysis of an already given situation, and the chaos has never been literally true: the sphericity due to νοῦς has always been present in fact; but partly also that Plato has accepted from Empedocles[3] the denial of a void and the assumption of a spherical οὐρανός.

With Plato's refusal to allow an ἔσχατος κύκλος in any way distinct from the rest of the sphere arises the difficulty of the composite motions of the masses of the four bodies which this passage purports to solve. The περίοδος τοῦ παντός means literally, it seems, the rotation of the sphere in every particle—for this motion reaches down to the centre, and the earth only remains still relatively to the οὐρανός because it has its own countervailing "winding" motion

---

[1] 51a.

[2] *Comm.* p. 398. Plato's ὑποδοχή does not, however, raise the difficulties of Aristotle's διάκενα (*v. ib.* pp. 675, 676). The διάκενα of 58b seem to be due to mere incidents of the transformation process and to the stereometrical facts that of the four solids only cubes and tetrahedra can be continuous and that rectilinear solids cannot fill a sphere.

[3] Ultimately from Parmenides, but the purely physical doctrines probably came through Empedocles rather than from a materialist interpretation of Parmenides by Plato.

to bring against it.[1] But if we consider the working of this rotation and the separating effect of the πλανωμένη αἰτία, their combined effect should be four revolving concentric spheres of fire, air, water and earth, which may explain the impossibility of "flying off to infinity" but certainly does not save the appearances. It is here that φιλία enters in with its Empedoclean (and ultimately Orphic) associations. Earlier in the dialogue we have been told how from the construction of the four elementary bodies in mathematical proportion the universe arose: τὸ τοῦ κόσμου σῶμα ἐγεννήθη δι' ἀναλογίας ὁμολογῆσαν φιλίαν τε ἔσχεν ἐκ τούτων, ὥστε εἰς ταὐτὸν αὑτῷ συνελθὸν ἄλυτον ὑπό του ἄλλου πλὴν ὑπὸ τοῦ συνδήσαντος γενέσθαι[2] (cf. 31 c supr.: δεσμῶν δὲ κάλλιστος ὃς ἂν αὐτὸν καὶ τὰ συνδούμενα ὅτι μάλιστα ἓν ποιῇ). This φιλία was perhaps a Pythagorean refinement on the Empedoclean moving power, Φιλότης, powerful in the limbs of mortals as in the frame of the universe. Now, however, there seems to be an appeal to the old conception of ἔρως as συναγωγεύς,[3] and we find an inward urge as well as revolution counteracting the dissipation wrought by ἀνάγκη. νοῦς assumes the character and function of φιλία as well as its own power to set up rotation, and so there is a constant tendency toward the μεῖγμα as well as, and greater than, the tendency towards the reign of νεῖκος. Thus the persuasion of ἀνάγκη by νοῦς is a situation very close to the world ἐπὶ τῆς Φιλότητος, when νεῖκος still persisted but did not prevail.

No doubt this interpretation reads much into σφίγγει. But we can hardly suppose Plato less aware of the main phenomena to be saved than we are, and we have seen that rotation and the shaking of the Receptacle do not together account for the actual interfusion

---

[1] Cornford, op. cit. p. 130. Whether ἱλλομένην at 40c init. means more than the simple countervailing of the οὐρανός seems to me still open to question, but that it does mean this, and that it means it because the rotation of the κυκλοφορία operates from the centre to the extremity Cornford has, I think, established beyond doubt.   [2] Tim. 32c.

[3] Konrat Ziegler in his article "Menschen- und Weltenwerden", which we have already quoted (Neue Jahrbücher (1913), pp. 529 sqq.), gives evidence for Orphic originals both of Empedocles and of Aristophanes's speech in the Symposium.

of the four bodies. If Plato could take over the ῥιζώματα and, to some degree, νεῖκος, and if he followed Empedocles in an implied denial of void, why should he refuse to bring into his cosmos the old binding force of φιλία, as Empedocles had done, when the phenomena demanded it?

CHAPTER V

THE GENERAL INTERPRETATION
OF THE *TIMAEUS*

The time has now come when one may without further explanation
reject outright Taylor's interpretation of the nature and purpose
of the *Timaeus*, while at the same time acknowledging fully in
common with all who study Plato the vast assistance its author has
brought to their study.[1] The rejection of Taylor's thesis is vital to
our present claim that Plato's doctrine of κίνησις, which had been
developing through the preceding dialogues in the manner we set
out to trace, comes to mature expression in the *Timaeus*. If the
dialogue were only a compendium of historical information concerning Empedoclean biology and Pythagorean mathematics, we
should have to leap from the *Philebus* to the *Laws* for our evidence
of Plato's doctrine of motion. But we hope to show that no such
leap is required; and moreover that in the *Laws*, especially in the
tenth book, we have a less exact expansion of what has been expressed
already in the *Philebus* and the *Timaeus*, and not that account with
a distinctively "scientific" character which Burnet was ready to
find there.[2]

Our examination of the antecedents in the pre-Socratic schools
of the κίνησις-doctrine of the *Timaeus* has led us to find little that is
distinctively Pythagorean. But we do find that Plato has selected
his material from these earlier writers in order to satisfy certain
a priori requirements of his own thought. There is a kind of
μαιευτική here not unlike that attributed to Socrates in the *Theaetetus*.[3]

[1] Some excuse for taking this attitude without a justifying explanation
will be found in the Preface. I would refer also to Professor G. C. Field's
review of Professor Taylor's commentary in *Mind*, vol. xxxviii.
[2] Ch. vii *infr.*
[3] I owe this suggestion to Mr H. C. Baldry. Emil Weerts in "Plato und
der Heraklitismus" (*Philologus*, Supplementband xxiii, p. 59) argues
that the μαιευτική of the *Theaetetus* differs from that of the historical
Socrates as revealed in the Socratic dialogues of Plato and in the
Alcibiades of Aeschines of Sphettus.

Socrates would attend his young men in their travail, being now past bearing himself. Plato will not so much bring forth a new philosophy of his own as extract from the existing systems by a truly Socratic technique the elements of truth they contain and will reject anything that has the nature of the "changeling". In the *Timaeus* Plato deals so with the early thinkers who had been ἐγκύμονες on matters of astronomy, physics and medicine—in fact περὶ φύσεως. And yet we find that he has in fact done more. He is really responsible for the form of the synthesis: they have supplied only the matter.

This "form" is the scheme of being into which everything must be fitted. This is remarkably close to the so-called "metaphysical" passage in the *Philebus* which we have studied already.[1] There the αἰτία is called τὸ ποιοῦν and τὸ δημιουργοῦν. The imagery in the *Timaeus* is that of model and copy, and there is now a stress laid on the εἴδη which reappear in their ancient role as the eternal "separate" models according to which the Δημιουργός must perform his creative work. There is the same insistence that the αἰτία is ὄντως ὄν like the εἴδη, but the figure of the Δημιουργός makes clear for the first time how the functioning of the αἰτία is related to the εἴδη. The αἰτία effects γένεσις after the pattern of the εἴδη. To do this it must be of the same degree of "reality" as the εἴδη. There is never any question of the αἰτία, the Δημιουργός himself, being bound up in any way with time as is the World-Soul he creates. This ultimate ἀρχὴ κινήσεως, "difficult to discover and impossible to publish to men", we must leave in his eternity while we consider the universe he has created, insisting only that its soul, and all the lesser souls, are less than their creator in their createdness but share his power to behold the εἴδη and are in their own sphere δημιουργοί. Plato has more than Aristotle's fifty-five moving Intelligences in his οὐρανός, but they are both subordinate and subservient, in so far as they remain intelligent, to "the Leader of all that moves", whose work was described in the *Politicus* myth and whose life was there said to be one of αὐτὸ ἑαυτὸ στρέφειν ἀεί—that which nothing bodily and created can achieve.[2]

[1] *V.* pp. 27 sqq. *supr.*   [2] p. 25 *supr.*

If we accept the οὐρανός as created with soul and body and now existing, we can go on to consider how the κινήσεις of the visible universe are related to its soul and how astronomy, ethics and psychophysics are fused and welded together into a unity within which all the detail must find its place. As for this detail, while Plato does not vouch for it all, he does imply that there is a standard of "scientific truth" by which it can be tested—it is the criterion of the εἰκὼς λόγος.

Now εἰκώς has been taken to mean no more than "probable": Taylor seems to have found an allusion to the "provisional and progressive nature of science" in it.[1] But this is to leave out of account the obvious connection of εἰκώς with εἰκών and to deny Plato the right to be his own interpreter. The passages in which the phrase εἰκὼς λόγος occurs are bound up with statements of the underlying metaphysic upon which the whole dialogue is built, and this can hardly be fortuitous.[2] We are reminded of εἰκόνες and εἴδωλα in other dialogues, particularly in the *Sophistes*. The sophist proffers εἴδωλα λεγόμενα περὶ πάντων and his art is εἰδωλοποιϊκή.[3] But there is such an art as εἰκαστική, which represents the true proportions of the original. We may suppose, then, that a true and a false science exist, and are related as are εἰκαστική and φανταστική in a later passage in the *Sophistes*.[4] The work of the true scientist is to substitute the former for the latter. But the philosopher is this true scientist, for if he has assimilated the circles in his head to the circles of the οὐρανός, the Circle of the Different in him will "run true" and the result will be δόξαι καὶ πίστεις βέβαιοι καὶ ἀληθεῖς.[5]

For the οὐρανός is an εἰκών, a copy in the realm of γένεσις of the αὐτόζῳον in the realm of ὄν, actuated by the World-Soul, which by reason of its construction is qualified to know the model and actuate the copy. We may leave aside the question how far the

---

[1] See Field's criticism, *Mind*, XXXVIII, pp. 93, 94.
[2] After its occurrence in the exordium of the creation story (29c) the phrase recurs at 48d, 53d *fin.*, 54a, 55d.
[3] *Soph.* 234c sqq.
[4] *Soph.* 266d *fin.*   [5] *Tim.* 37b, 44b.

construction of the world-soul is mythical, pointing out the one supremely important respect in which the soul when constructed is related to Being as it is described in the most metaphysical of Plato's works, the *Sophistes*. Cornford's explanation of the composition of the World-Soul in terms of the *Sophistes* ontology has settled the place of the *Timaeus* as a critical dialogue and explained why its cosmology takes the form it does. Taylor offers as a general explanation of what the construction of the ἁρμονία is meant to teach that if ψυχή is to find system in things it must first have system in itself, and if it is to put system in things it must itself be a system. "As regards its formal structure, the soul which knows the laws and proportions of all things is a thing which has an intrinsic law of proportion in its own constitution."[1] This is all good Pythagoreanism and is accepted by Plato in the *Timaeus*, but there are two specific applications of this general principle neither of which comes from Pythagorean sources, and in combining them Plato is doing more than any Pythagorean, fifth-century or fourth-century, could have done. First the soul is so constructed as to answer to and cognise the structure of the world of Forms as Plato had come to picture it in the *Sophistes*, pervaded by the character of Same and Other. Then the actual processes by which this cognition is constantly effected are shown to be such as can be represented or imaged on the visible plane by the astronomical scheme of οὐρανός and planets moving with contrary motions. So the fusion is made between ontology, epistemology, psychophysics and astronomy and we justify the final encomium of the οὐρανός as ζῷον ὁρατὸν τὰ ὁρατὰ περιέχον, εἰκὼν τοῦ νοητοῦ θεὸς αἰσθητός, μέγιστος καὶ ἄριστος κάλλιστός τε καὶ τελεώτατος.[2]

We can see how this achievement of a rational cosmology depends on the insight that Same and Other could be "bodied forth" in Ouranos and ecliptic. This gives final sanction to astronomy as the science to awake man to his divine destiny, and justifies the time and thought that the Academy was lavishing upon it. It makes astronomy rank higher than psychology and physics. Alcmaeon had provided Plato with the means of bridging the distance between

[1] Taylor, *Comm.* p. 159.   [2] 92 c.

the world-soul and the human soul. Alcmaeon had simply said man's soul was immortal because it moved constantly like the heavenly bodies. Plato now seizes upon this and gives every human head the psychic motions which by their operation in the world-soul give rise to the abiding celestial movements. The Empedoclean physics must take a subordinate place, though it is allowed to introduce another moving cause and another form of motion, the chaotic σεισμός, which must, indeed, be introduced to "save the phenomena" of physics and biology at all.

Taylor's contention that Plato knew of the theory of Eudoxus when he wrote the *Timaeus* but deliberately excluded it from the dialogue because it was anachronistic to make a fifth-century Pythagorean expound it is perhaps the most convincing argument in support of his general thesis; for there is reason to ask why Plato clung to the older Pythagorean astronomy when the astronomical thinking of the Academy was moving so quickly, as the work of Eudoxus and Heraclides shows it to have moved.[1] The answer surely is that while Plato had no reason for preferring one astronomical scheme to another as such, there is every reason to think that he would regard that older Pythagorean astronomy as the only "probable" one. It is the εἰκὼς λόγος, the account of the true εἰκών of the World-Soul with its two circles of Same and Other.

This is evident if we consider the actual astronomies available to him. The Ionian systems he would set aside at once. He rejected the Anaxagorean scheme as materialist and mechanist and the Atomist astronomy would have been (or was, if he knew it) re-

[1] The much discussed passage in the *Epinomis* (988 b), where Burnet introduces an οὐκ into the text and Taylor, though not consenting to this, still interprets the passage as meaning that Plato did *not* believe that the οὐρανός carries round the planets, is perhaps to be understood as reflecting the contemporary controversies in the Academy. Perhaps some members of it were prepared to argue for the retention of the οὐρανός in the old sense, even at the expense of being told "they knew very little about it". Plato would be in sympathy with these conservatives; though there is perhaps a trace in this passage of a shaking of his certainty (if the *Epinomis* is genuine) which might give rise to the stories of a μεταμέλεια reported by Plutarch.

pellent to him for the same reasons: it found in the heavens motions totally incapable of expressing the ἄπαυστος καὶ ἔμφρων βίος of the Ouranos. This leaves us with the astronomies being discussed in the Academy at the time, especially those of Eudoxus and of the central fire.

Eudoxus's theory was probably worked out in response to the πρόβλημα laid down by Plato himself:[1] τίνων ὑποτεθεισῶν ὁμαλῶν καὶ τεταγμένων κινήσεων διασωθῇ τὰ περὶ τῆς κινήσεως τῶν πλανω- μένων φαινόμενα; The fact that it was the planetary anomalies that Plato was seeking to account for indicates his anxiety to maintain the double-motion astronomy while saving the phenomena. But Eudoxus's elaborate solution could not meet the case for Plato, for it was not an εἰκών of the World-Soul. He could not allow that the soul moving the Ouranos was a host of movents at cross purposes, some moving starless spheres, others moving spheres with lifeless stars fixed to them. We naturally contrast Aristotle's attitude. He had no *a priori* reasons for refusing Eudoxus's scheme. He did not believe in a single world-soul whose activities were represented by the Ouranos and the ecliptic. He will have nothing to do with the notion that thought is circular.[2] The movers of his spheres were unmoved, the spheres themselves were capable of spherical movement by nature. So he is at liberty to postulate as many movers as the facts require, and he goes to Eudoxus and Callippus for these facts. Plato does none of these things, but not as an archaist: he refuses the scheme because it is not for him an εἰκὼς λόγος in the sense we have defined.

But if Eudoxus's scheme was not an εἰκὼς λόγος, still less was the "central-fire" astronomy. For one of the main difficulties in eluci- dating this theory is to decide what motion it can allow to the Ouranos. Sir Thomas Heath has pointed out[3] that it must have given it *some* motion, and offers the suggestion that it was either an indefinitely fast rotation of the whole universe or an imperceptibly slow motion. In either case the motion would not satisfy Plato as

[1] Simplicius on Ar. *De Caelo* 293 a 4, from Eudemus.
[2] *De Anima* A 3, 407 a 15 sqq.; cf. p. 83 *infr.* Cf. Simpl. *ad loc.* p. 44, ll. 6 sqq.
[3] *Aristarchus of Samos*, pp. 101 sqq.

a description of the effects of the world-soul, for the Circle of the Same "has the mastery" over the Circle of the Other and the νυχθήμερον is ἡ τῆς μιᾶς καὶ φρονιμωτάτης κυκλήσεως περίοδος.[1] On the assumptions of the central-fire theory this could not be so: therefore Plato must reject it, and we have no conclusive evidence that he ever broke with the geocentric astronomy which was his one εἰκὼς λόγος.

Within this Ouranos, however, the interplay of the two αἰτίαι κινήσεως, νοῦς and ἀνάγκη, is more important than the workings of the astronomical system. We have the τρίτον γένος added to our account of the universe at 52b 2, but we must recognise over and above the three kinds—ὄν, γένεσις, χώρα—the two αἰτίαι κινήσεως, νοῦς and the πλανωμένη αἰτία. We must remember that αἰτία never means a previous event related causally to a subsequent, but an active agency of a higher order of reality which is literally "responsible for" the physical event.[2] We must go on to examine the physical motions for which the two causes are thus responsible.

NOTE ON THE "CENTRAL FIRE" ASTRONOMY

It has become accepted nowadays that this doctrine is plainly fourth-century. Burnet thinks that it may have arisen from certain views of Empedocles. Frank is prepared to be definite concerning its date (*Plato und die sogenannten Pythagoreer*, pp. 278 sqq.):[3]

"Die Zeit dieses astronomischen Systems ist...durch die Nachricht Theophrasts auch klar genug bestimmt, dass es von Plato erst in seiner letzten Zeit angenommen wurde. Nach Platos Tode haben es dann fast alle seine Schüler, sowohl Speusipp als Philippus von Opus und Herakleides von Pontus vertreten, es ist also tatsächlich die offizielle Lehre der platonischen Akademie in der Zeit des Aristoteles gewesen. Vorher findet sich keine Spur davon und

---

[1] 39c *init*. The κράτος of the Circle of the Same implies a definite period of motion and a swifter one than the planets. Their achievement of the τέλεος ἐνιαυτός is measured τῷ ταὐτοῦ καὶ ὁμοίως ἰόντος κύκλῳ.

[2] Cf. αἰτία ἑλομένου, ὁ δὲ θεὸς ἀναίτιος, *Rep.* x 617e.

[3] Cornford exposes the weakness of Frank's evidence at p. 129 n. 2 of his *Commentary*.

andererseits scheint es schon von der nächsten Generation der Akademie, von Xenocrates wieder aufgegeben worden zu sein, wobei vielleicht die heftigen dagegen gerichteten Angriffe des Aristoteles nicht ohne Einfluss waren."

Taylor also suggests (*Comm.* p. 237) that the *Timaeus* theory of the oscillation of the earth was a "half-way stage" to the central-fire theory.

This is a complete reversal of former views which based themselves more unquestioningly on Aristotle's statements in *Metaphysics* A.[1] Martin had to contend in his day for the recognition of the geocentric scheme as Pythagorean at all (*Études*, II, p. 107). But it is perhaps worth enquiring whether the modern view has reacted farther than the evidence warrants. Allowing that the historical Philolaus probably held the geocentric view (*Phaedo* 108e; Burnet, *E. G. Ph.*[3] p. 297) and that no weight as evidence attaches to the "fragments of Philolaus" which led later writers to call the hypothesis "Philolaic", this does not necessarily disprove its antiquity.[2]

It may be that while the scheme prevailed as a scientific hypothesis only at the time that Frank defines, it nevertheless had a history in the Brotherhood. Aristotle does not describe it in terms that suggest it is merely recent. His reference to the reasons for the ἀντίχθων[3] may not be a mere jest but a reference to some early form of the doctrine. The mythological names for the central fire need not "blind us to the fact that we are dealing with a scientific hypothesis" (Burnet, *op. cit.* p. 299 *init.*), but they do point to an earlier stage in its history. Simplicius's comment on Aristotle, *De Caelo* B 13, incorporating as it does a fragment from Aristotle's own work on the Pythagoreans (Simpl. 511, 26), strongly confirms the evidence for this view. The reference here to the δημιουργικὴ δύναμις of the central fire suggests the parallel to the passage in the

---

[1] A 5, 986 a 8–13.

[2] We must also give up all attempt to find the scheme in the *Phaedrus* myth, at any rate in any explicit form. Martin (*Études*, II, p. 114) brings forward excellent arguments in this connection, against Cousin, who followed the anonymous *Life of Pythagoras*. But it is more pardonable to identify Ἑστία with the central fire than to identify her with the earth in the geocentric scheme as M. Robin appears to do in his unfortunate footnote on the passage in his edition of the dialogue in the Budé series (p. 37 n.).

[3] The ἀντίχθων pre-supposes the central fire, and the whole scheme is regarded as primitive Pythagoreanism contemporary with the magical faith in the δέκας.

Metaphysics (N 3, 1091a 13 sqq.) where the One, here the fiery nucleus, limits the unlimited by breathing in the boundless air. The "central fire" astronomy really descends from this cosmology, which Aristotle admits to have been intended as physical even while arguing that it is really mathematical. The early controversy as to whether the world breathes probably centres round some cosmology of this kind rather than the geocentric astronomy of Pythagoras and Alcmaeon.

But it suffices for the purpose of the argument of the foregoing chapter if a theory which made the earth a planet and so abolished the diurnal rotation of the οὐρανός was a live option for Plato when he wrote the *Timaeus*. Only a combination of Taylor's hypothesis with Frank's would render that argument inadmissible.

CHAPTER VI

ΝΟΥΣ AND ΑΝΑΓΚΗ AS ΑΙΤΙΑΙ ΚΙΝΗΣΕΩΣ IN THE *TIMAEUS*

When the new beginning is made at *Timaeus* 47c we are told that we must study the nature of the motion set up by the errant cause (τὸ τῆς πλανωμένης αἰτίας ᾗ φέρειν πέφυκεν). Nothing so explicit is said concerning the motions set up by νοῦς, though we were told at 34a that the Demiurge gave the οὐρανός the motion most appropriate to its body, the one out of all the seven most bound up with mind and intelligence. It remains to set out briefly the motions involved in the οὐρανός as it now is, as a "going concern". We may best bring out all the factors if we consider these types of motion in three contrasting pairs: (*a*) the psychic motions of the αἰτίαι and the mechanical motions of the συναίτια; (*b*) the contrasting circular motions representing the Circles of Same and Other in the Soul of the οὐρανός; and (*c*) the κυκλοφορία arising from νοῦς and the σεισμός arising from ἀνάγκη.

(*a*) αἰτίαι *and* συναίτια

The distinction between αἰτίαι and συναίτια goes back to the prison-scene in the *Phaedo* and appears again in the distinction between the πρωτουργοὶ and the δευτερουργοὶ κινήσεις in the *Laws*.[1] The συναίτια in the *Phaedo* were the bones and sinews that kept the body of Socrates in Athens in obedience to his choice of the best. The συναίτια of the *Timaeus* and of the *Laws* are not to be otherwise understood, though here the bones and sinews of Socrates are analysed further into "cooling and heating or compacting and rarefying agents"[2] in the *Timaeus*, and yet more fully in the *Laws* into "increase and diminution, combination and separation, and the characters of heat and cold, weight and lightness, hardness and

[1] *Laws* x 896c 7 sqq.; *Phaedo* 99a 4.
[2] *Tim.* 46d 2.

softness, white and black, sour and sweet, which follow upon these".[1]
The essential point for Plato is that they are all συναίτια, which
give the "how" but not the "why", and the essence of his quarrel
with the followers of Archelaus and the Heracliteans is that they
regard causes of this order as competent to give an exhaustive
account of the universe.

The real drama of the universe lies for Plato in the conflict of the
αἰτίαι. The physical motions are all soul-caused, and there is no
question of recalcitrance on their part. They obey orders: the whole
question is whether νοῦς or ἀνάγκη commands. It is this drama,
Aeschylean no doubt,[2] which is faithfully reflected in the visible
motions of the οὐρανός. "The coming-into-being of this universe
was a compromise begotten of the wrestling of mind and necessity"
seems to be the sense of 48a _init._; for σύστασις has not lost its
military colour.[3] Moreover, since we cannot take the creation in
time literally, it is a conflict that is always going on. This does not
necessitate our regarding ἀνάγκη as an evil world-soul antagonistic
to νοῦς or even a deliberately refractory element in the world-soul.
It is simply "a factor which confronts the divine Reason and is
neither ordained nor completely controlled by it"[4]—it needs to be
persuaded, and does not "consent" to the co-existence of dense
bone and much flesh, for example.[5]

The strict distinction between αἰτίαι and συναίτια tends to be
confused with the distinction between νοῦς and ἀνάγκη, and here
the real confusion is always of ἀνάγκη with the συναίτια. This
confusion seems to arise once in Cornford's account of Reason and
Necessity[6] and at one point also in his account of the chaotic motions
of the Receptacle.[7] In the former discussion (and in subsequent
controversy with Professor Taylor in _Mind_[8]) he appears to attribute
the unhappy fact that brittleness must go with hardness (and that
therefore men are liable to fracture their bones) to the inherent

[1] _Laws_ x 897a 5 sqq.   [2] Cornford, _op. cit._ Epilogue, pp. 361 sqq.
[3] There seems to be no sexual meaning. ἀνάγκη is not the female partner—
still less does she supply the matter only, as Bäumker seems to suggest.
[4] Cornford, _op. cit._ p. 209.   [5] _Ib._ p. 175; _v. infr._
[6] _Ib._ pp. 174, 175.   [7] _Ib._ p. 209, para. 1.
[8] _Mind_, XLVII, pp. 180–199, 321–330.

defects and incompatibilities of the material qualities, in face of
which the Demiurge has to choose the less of two evils. But this
is surely not the whole story. Even at this point Plato tries to hold
to his explanation of a psychic cause of all phenomena. It was
ἀνάγκη that refused to concede the point to νοῦς, refusing in this
case to "bring everything to the best possible". When νοῦς requested
of ἀνάγκη a suitable mechanism for ὄψις this was granted: in the
present case the request was refused. The Demiurge thereupon
realised that to force the point would be to dislocate the general
system of pairs of qualities that ἀνάγκη was willing to tolerate, and
so, rather than press the special need at the general expense, it
accepted the present arrangement. This view makes ἀνάγκη "behind"
τὸ σαρκῶδες and τὸ νευρῶδες the real obstacle to the teleological
planning of νοῦς, and this seems to be intended by the careful phrase
ἡ ἐξ ἀνάγκης γιγνομένη καὶ συντρεφομένη φύσις at 75 a 7.

In the same way, we are surely meant to suppose that there *is*
a psychic cause for the shaking of the Receptacle described at 53 a.
Cornford seems to deny any soul to the chaos before the creation,
refusing the view of Plutarch and Atticus "that the soul of the
world was at first irrational, having only the irrational motions,
and then the Demiurge endowed it with reason and reduced it to
order".[1] Surely there "was" such an irrational soul just as much
(and just as little) as there "was" a chaos of unformed aggregates
of the four bodies moving at random with clashing powers. Plutarch
and Atticus may be wrong in treating the account as literal history,
but they are right in their insistence that soul is the cause of all
motions. The clashing "powers" of which Cornford speaks are
"consequent upon" the characters of the four simple formations,
which are still unformed while God is absent from the world. Hot
and cold as distinct qualities depend upon the triangular construction.
But "traces" of qualities like "traces" of the four bodies were in

[1] Cornford, *op. cit.* p. 203. Cf. Plut. *De Animae Procr.* 1015 d *fin.*: ὁ γὰρ
Πλάτων μητέρα μὲν καὶ τιθήνην καλεῖ τὴν ὕλην, αἰτίαν δὲ κακοῦ τὴν
κινητικὴν τῆς ὕλης καὶ περὶ τὰ σώματα γιγνομένην μεριστὴν ἄτακτον
καὶ ἄλογον οὐκ ἄψυχον δὲ κίνησιν,...ψυχὴ γὰρ αἰτία κινήσεως καὶ
ἀρχή, νοῦς δὲ τάξεως καὶ συμφωνίας περὶ κίνησιν. ὁ γὰρ θεὸς οὐκ ἀνέστησε
τὴν ὕλην ἀργοῦσαν ἀλλ' ἔστησεν ὑπὸ τῆς ἀνοήτου ταραττομένην αἰτίας.

the chaos—that is to say these physical powers are not ultimately tolerant of rational explanation, but the command of them is taken over by νοῦς from ἀνάγκη in so far as they enter into the cosmic scheme and follow rational laws. The chaotic σεισμός no longer has control, but it persists as a factor in the οὐρανός and it "was", and is, due directly to ἀνάγκη.

The confusion between the two antitheses νοῦς—ἀνάγκη and αἰτία—συναίτια is nowhere more evident than at 46d 5 sqq.: τῶν γὰρ ὄντων ᾧ νοῦν μόνῳ κτᾶσθαι προσήκει λεκτέον ψυχήν—τοῦτο δὲ ἀόρατον, πῦρ δὲ καὶ ὕδωρ καὶ γῆ καὶ ἀὴρ σώματα πάντα ὁρατὰ γέγονεν, τὸν δὲ νοῦ καὶ ἐπιστήμης ἐραστὴν ἀνάγκη τὰς τῆς ἔμφρονος φύσεως αἰτίας πρώτας μεταδιώκειν, ὅσαι δ᾽ ὑπ᾽ ἄλλων μὲν κινουμένων ἕτερα δ᾽ ἐξ ἀνάγκης κινούντων γίγνονται δευτέρας. ποιητέον δὴ κατὰ ταῦτα καὶ ἡμῖν· λεκτέα μὲν ἀμφότερα τὰ τῶν αἰτιῶν γένη, χωρὶς δὲ ὅσαι μετὰ νοῦ καλῶν καὶ ἀγαθῶν δημιουργοὶ καὶ ὅσαι μονωθεῖσαι φρονήσεως τὸ τυχὸν ἄτακτον ἑκάστοτε ἐξεργάζονται. Here the opposition of τῆς ἔμφρονος φύσεως and ὅσαι... γίγνονται seems to be that between psychic as such and physical as such. But this is not really the case, as appears on closer inspection, for the genitives κινουμένων and κινούντων really depend on αἰτίαι understood before γίγνονται, and then we see that this clause is the true parallel to τὰς τῆς ἔμφρονος φύσεως. We study the causes of the rational in nature first, the causes of the irrational second. ὑπ᾽ ἄλλων μὲν κινούμενα ἕτερα δ᾽ ἐξ ἀνάγκης κινοῦντα are those physical processes which serve no rational end, or rather that element in all physical process which fails to do so, and their cause is precisely ἀνάγκη: ἐξ ἀνάγκης is explanatory much in the same way as ἔμφρονος. The two classes of αἰτίαι are then summed up, the second class being now clearly psychical though irrational—ὅσαι μονωθεῖσαι φρονήσεως τὸ τυχὸν ἄτακτον ἑκάστοτε ἐξεργάζονται.

Thus we must draw the double distinction, in the language of *Laws* x, between πρωτουργοὶ and δευτερουργοὶ κινήσεις on the one hand but also between ψυχὴ νοῦν προσλαβοῦσα and ψυχὴ ἀνοίᾳ συγγενομένη on the other.[1] The συναίτια of the *Timaeus* and the δευτερουργοὶ κινήσεις of the *Laws* can be said ὑπηρετεῖν (*Tim.*

[1] *Laws* x 897a, b.

46c *fin.*) in two senses. They are in any case subservient to psychic causes, for only soul can maintain them at all; but they are also subservient in that they must obey the dictates of the soul while the soul is living its own life of "wish, reflection, foresight, counsel, judgment—true or false—pleasure, pain, hope, fear, hate, love".[1] These are the soul's proper motions, and the body obeys in the sense that the bones and sinews of Socrates take him over the frontier, or keep him in prison, according to his choice of the best.

(b) The motions of the Same and the Different

Proclus was prepared to see an analogy between the two contrary revolutions of the Ouranos in the *Politicus* myth and the contrary movements of the circles of the Same and the Other in the World-Soul in the *Timaeus*. Cornford accepts this analogy and supports it from the account of the circles of the soul in infancy;[2] but closer consideration of the passages concerned may well lead us to see the πλάνη due to the σύμφυτος ἐπιθυμία as the factor which perverts the Circle of the Different and not the force which constitutes the Circle itself. We shall have to judge the exact relation between the πλανῆται and the πλανωμένη αἰτία with this consideration in view.

The construction of the World-Soul brings together the metaphysical results of the *Sophistes* and the double-motion astronomy, as we have seen. The Circle of the Different is an integral part of the World-Soul in its unity, and is "split into seven unequal circles" only in its physical manifestations in order to save the planetary phenomena. In cognition, in the world-soul and in the human soul alike, the Circle of the Different is concerned with sense-percepts, but we are told at 37b that a true account can be given "concerning the Different" as well as "concerning the Same". When the circle of the Different runs true there arise "judgments and beliefs that are valid and true", and these are a real part of cognition, though secondary to the "rational understanding and knowledge" that arise from the proper functioning of the Circle of the Same. The Circle of the Different is in no sense irrational, except in the sense

---

[1] *Laws* 897a *init.* tr. Taylor.
[2] Cornford, *op. cit.* p. 208 (Proclus, *Comm.* I 289). Cf. *ib.* p. 76.

that its province is the sub-rational; but its function is to bring the sub-rational as near to rationality as it can be brought. It was with both circles that the World-Soul made its "divine beginning of ceaseless *and intelligent* life for all time".[1]

Turning next to the distresses of the soul in infancy,[2] we find that the attacking forces from outside "shake the soul-circles violently; they run counter to the Circle of the Same, obstructing its course and overthrowing its control, and they dislocate the Circle of the Different". The trouble is that the Circle of the Different no longer "runs true" (ὀρθὸς ἰών 37b) but is forced into twists and turns in which it behaves as if its motions were rectilinear, like those of the assailing particles, instead of circular. There is nothing in the first half of the dialogue to contradict and much to confirm the association of circular motion with rationality and of rectilinear motion with πλάνη. The οὐρανός is made ἀπλανής in respect of the six rectilinear motions.[3] We must restore the "circles that have wandered" in us till they are ἀπλανεῖς, that is until they are as perfectly circular as the circle of the World-Soul itself.[4]

But however true this may be of the soul-circles, is it not the case that the physical motions of the planets do exhibit the influence of the πλανωμένη αἰτία?[5] Both the *Timaeus* and the *Laws* in a much-disputed passage in the seventh book[6] show that Plato wished to assert the contrary, and to vindicate the planets from the charge of wandering. When the planets themselves are first introduced,[7] Plato himself calls them simply ἄστρα and treats the common appellation πλανητά as an undeserved soubriquet (ἐπίκλην ἔχοντα πλανητά) since they are regular enough in fact to act as the clocks of the universe and "define and preserve the numbers of Time". Men cannot read the time by these clocks, save in the case of the solar year

---

[1] *Tim.* 36e, tr. Cornford.   [2] *Tim.* 43a sqq.

[3] *Tim.* 34a 1 sqq. "Rectilinear" is used as the contrary of circular and implies no specific "direction" like the "natural" up and down of the motions of the ἁπλᾶ σώματα of Aristotle.

[4] *Tim.* 43e 3 sqq.

[5] Burnet and Taylor point out the connection between πλανῆται and πλανωμένη αἰτία. *V.* Taylor, *Comm.* p. 191.

[6] *Laws* VII 822a.   [7] *Tim.* 38c.

and lunar month, but they are nevertheless regular.¹ At 40b also, after the account of the fixed stars, exempt from all motions save divine rotation and forward movement under control of the Same, the planets are brought in as τὰ τρεπόμενα καὶ πλάνην τοιαύτην ἴσχοντα—"having turnings and, to this extent, wanderings".² But the whole point is to assimilate them to the fixed stars as far as possible and to point out that their apparently rectilinear reversals of motion at their turnings are only the effect of the motion of the Same turning their circles into spirals. The passage at *Laws* VII 822a it seems best to take simply as an amplification of this, though in a more verbose and less exact form; just as we shall find a summary of the *Timaeus* account of the motions of the οὐρανός in the account of the ten "kinds" of motion in the tenth book of the *Laws*. Men say the planets "wander" and mistake the slower for the swifter simply because they do not understand the double-motion astronomy as it is worked out in the *Timaeus*.³

It is for this reason that it may after all be right to find some meaning of ἰλλομένην in the famous sentence at 40b *fin.* concerning the motion of the earth which makes of it rather more than the countervailing of the motion of the οὐρανός and the "guardianship" thereby of night and day.⁴ We must remember that the complications of the planetary motions arise from the necessity of keeping the Circle of the Other as their norm. The astronomical facts must show forth the perfect course of this Circle in the visible world. But the facts are recalcitrant. The Circle must be split into seven to begin with. Then the phenomena of station and retrogradation

¹ 39c, d.   ² Cornford, *op. cit.* p. 118 n. 3.
³ *Laws* VII 822a; Cornford, *op. cit.* pp. 89–91. I now feel bound to accept Cornford's interpretation of this passage, though the difficulty of οὔτε νέος οὔτε πάλαι ἀκηκοώς at 821e remains, and we can make nothing in this connection of the passages in Plutarch which speak of Plato's late repentance for his assignment of the central place to the earth (*Plat. Qu.* 1006c; *Vita Numae* XI). The phrase οὔτε νέος κ.τ.λ. is, however, puzzling on any view. At 819d the Athenian declares that he was told "quite recently" that there are incommensurable quantities! Such passages tempt one to the reverse of Taylor's and Burnet's opinion that a dramatic date early in the fifth century conditions the *Timaeus* but not the *Laws*.
⁴ Cornford, *op. cit.* pp. 130, 131.

must be accommodated to the theory, though they have no psychic cause save the self-will of the planets' souls. But all these refinements, while accounting for the varying "years" of the planets and the phenomena of station and retrogradation, could never account for variations in latitude. Could Plato admit such variations without implying that the World-Soul itself had its motions distorted like those of the human soul in infancy? There was an escape from this dilemma. The earth on the astronomical plane has no counterpart in the constitution of the soul. The common centre of the two bands is neglected: only the contrary senses and the κράτος of Same over Different enter into consideration. Therefore it is not impossible that Plato allowed displacements in latitude to the earth, to account for observed facts, which he could not admit in the planets without straining the vital link between astronomical orbits and circles in the World-Soul. If so, the earth is the only true "planet". True the earth, an ensouled goddess, ought to choose the purely circular path—in her case rotation only. But earth is pre-eminently the theatre of rectilinear motions due to ἀνάγκη, and if Plato had certain astronomical variations to account for, which he could not attribute to the planets, what was more natural than to argue that the earth, albeit "the first and most venerable of gods", shares the failings of other gods of tradition and is not completely persuaded to the good and wise path of Circularity?

There is, indeed, a kind of "order of merit" among the planets themselves. The sun has the place of honour because he alone presents the motion of the Circle of the Different unmodified.[1] He may be said to follow with it of his own volition just as the fixed stars "follow" the motion of the Same;[2] and so he shares their perfect rationality, we may assume. The rest of the planets with their ἐναντίαι δυνάμεις are by so much the less rational, and earth may descend, as we have seen, to an irrational oscillation. But whether this is so or no, we have good reason to confine the πλανωμένη αἰτία to departures from κυκλοφορία and not to see the Circle of the Other as the sphere of its operations. The σύμφυτος ἐπιθυμία

---

[1] Cornford, *op. cit.* pp. 83, 84; cf. *Epin.* 986e, there cited.
[2] 40a 5.

is now to be found operating like νεῖκος, in the σεισμός, which the rational motions of the World-Soul must conquer in order that both the circles may run true.

(c) κυκλοφορία *and* σεισμός

We are left, then, with two αἰτίαι, each having its own κίνησις in itself and each setting up a characteristic form of κίνησις among the four bodies: νοῦς the cause of κυκλοφορία and ἀνάγκη the cause of σεισμός. The four bodies themselves are equally capable of κυκλο-φορία and of σεισμός, though κυκλοφορία is superimposed upon σεισμός. The mistakes of interpretation in later times arose chiefly from supposing that κυκλοφορία could not be a motion of the four bodies and that σεισμός did not require an ulterior πλάνη of irration-ality in the πλανωμένη αἰτία to account for it.

All physical κυκλοφορία is organised by νοῦς: there can be no κυκλοφορία anywhere arising from ἀνάγκη. This condemns any theory of an irrational vortex, though it affirms with the necessary modifications the teaching of Anaxagoras on νοῦς and περιχώρησις. Even the apparent exception to the principle, the περίωσις of the circulation and the digestive and respiratory processes in man, is probably to be regarded as a kind of outworking of the soul-circles: in fact we are told as much at 42 c, where man is doomed to have no rest from the travail of transmigration until "letting the revolution of the same and uniform within himself *draw into its train* all that turmoil of fire and water and air and earth that had later grown about it, he should control its irrational turbulence by discourse of reason and return once more to the form of his first and best condition".[1] This condition is the constant condition of the stars: to them man must be assimilated as far as a mortal may. Since, however, man must eat to live as the stars need not, his best approach to their bliss in mortal life is to impose uniformity and proportion on the bodily processes.[2]

[1] tr. Cornford. This must surely be the right interpretation of συνεπισπώ-μενον and not the Bunyanesque one given by Taylor in his translation (p. 40 n. 1) that "the returning sinner has a burden to drag with him".
[2] *Tim.* 82 b.

All the four bodies, however, are capable of κυκλοφορία in obedience to νοῦς. The stars are made *mostly* of fire but not entirely,[1] and earth at the centre has a κυκλοφορία of its own in its countervailing of the motions of the οὐρανός. Similarly, fire is as subject to σεισμός arising from ἀνάγκη as any other body—it is, in fact, εὐκινητότατον.[2] The general account of σεισμός we have already considered in estimating the debt of Plato to Empedocles: it only remains to show how the subsequent criticisms define the *Timaeus* position by contrast.

Aristotle's direct criticism of the *Timaeus* account of the World-Soul in the *De Anima* (A 3; especially 407a 21–32) is partly vitiated by its failure to recognise that Plato does not regard all κίνησις as being, by definition, ἐν τόπῳ as Aristotle himself regards it. Plato does not in fact say that the motions of the heavens are identical with the motions of the soul (407a 1), and Proclus rightly claims that Plato does not make the soul a μέγεθος[3] as Aristotle here asserts. But he does say that the sphere well-turned is the best εἰκών of the motions of νοῦς: this νοῦ κίνησις is best called κυκλοφορία from the bodily motion it sets up. This is most carefully explained to the young men in *Laws* x in an important passage beginning τίνα οὖν νοῦ κίνησις...φύσιν ἔχει;[4] against this Aristotle argues that νόησις is neither κυκλοφορία nor *like* κυκλοφορία but achieves rather a συμπέρασμα.[5] This is the real break-away from Plato's thought, and defines it sharply. The Parmenidean relation between thought and sphericity which Plato kept to the end Aristotle abandoned. We need not follow the debate between Platonists and Aristotelians on

---

[1] *Tim.* 40a 2; *v.* Taylor, *Comm.* p. 222.

[2] *Tim.* 56a *fin.* The classification of the five creatures in the five regions in the *Epinomis* seems to represent a falling away from this position and perhaps raises more suspicion of the genuineness of the dialogue than anything else in it. The difficulty is sufficiently indicated in Mr Harward's note on *Epin.* 981d 7 (J. Harward, *The Epinomis of Plato*, p. 124): "As the whole passage is mythology it is perhaps not suitable to press the criticism that Plato was aware that the moon shone with reflected light and therefore ought to have given her the same στερεμνία φύσις as the earth."

[3] Procl. *In Tim.* II 279.　　　　[4] *Laws* x 897d 3 sqq.

[5] Ar. *De Anima* A 3, 407a 15 sqq.

the question "whether the soul is moved" which Macrobius gives us in his Commentary on the *Somnium Scipionis*, for it only elaborates the points that Aristotle's own criticism raises directly and Plato's defenders are not always his best friends.[1]

A frequent difficulty in the later discussions is the interpretation of the passage in the *Timaeus* where we are told that the Δημιουργός "set the World's Soul at its centre causing it to extend throughout the whole and also wrapped the world's body round with soul on the outside".[2] How far the αἰτίαι κινήσεως predominate in definite regions of the οὐρανός it is impossible to determine exactly. Certainly the κυκλοφορίαι of the stars, of the planets, and of human and animal ψυχαί do indicate localisations of ψυχή as well as individual centres of psychic activity. But all these manifestations are contained within the οὐρανός itself, which must, it is said, τὰ πάντα ζῷα ἐντὸς αὐτοῦ περιειληφέναι.[3] In considering the physical motions of the body of the οὐρανός as a whole, it would be dangerous to suppose that there is any particle of any of the four bodies in motion anywhere within it whose motion is not the resultant of the κυκλοφορία of νοῦς and the σεισμός of ἀνάγκη. With the κυκλοφορία goes the process described at 58a of σφίγγειν in which we have seen the survival of the Orphic ἔρως and the Empedoclean φιλία. Thus Plato is able to postulate one κίνησις, the σεισμός, instead of Aristotle's separate ἀρχαὶ κινήσεως in each of the ἁπλᾶ σώματα. Nor does he need any doctrine of "natural places", for the σεισμός has the effect of separating the bodies to the several regions in which they tend to predominate. He does, however, attribute to νοῦς the recombining tendency by which φιλία conquered νεῖκος in Empedocles, as well as its power to set up circular motion. Finally, and most important of all, he regards κυκλοφορία as a possible motion of the four bodies and regards it as extending throughout the whole οὐρανός from the centre to the extremity, overcoming the aimless σεισμός that ἀνάγκη would set up were the "persuasion of νοῦς" absent.

So all-pervading was the influence of Aristotle's doctrine that

[1] Macrobius *In Somn. Scip.* II 13 sqq.
[2] *Tim.* 34b; *v.* Taylor *ad loc. Comm.* p. 105.
[3] *Tim.* 39e.

the fifth body alone moves naturally in a circle that we find even Plutarch and Atticus misunderstanding the *Timaeus* doctrine. Plutarch in the *Platonicae Quaestiones*[1] at the end of an enquiry why Plato used rectilinear figures (the triangles) rather than cyclic for his geometrical figures says that the reason is that the motions of all perceived bodies are rectilinear, that τὸ σφαιροειδὲς οὔκ ἐστιν αἰσθητοῦ σώματος ἀλλὰ τῆς ψυχῆς καὶ τοῦ νοῦ στοιχεῖον, οἷς καὶ τὴν κυκλοφορικὴν κίνησιν ὡς προσήκουσαν κατὰ φύσιν ἀποδίδωσιν. Atticus the Platonist in the second century A.D. says that "Plato taught that the four bodies have each a natural, simple, rectilinear motion (fire to the circumference, earth to the centre, the other two to the intermediate regions) and he reserved circular motion to the soul. Aristotle practised a simple deception on himself by assigning the circular motion, as though it were a bodily one, to the 'fifth body' in the same way as he distributed the rectilinear motions among the other four."[2] Since these mistakes of interpretation arose from tacit acceptance of Aristotle's doctrine on the part of his critics,[3] there

[1] 1004c.   [2] Eusebius, *Praep. Evang.* XV 8, 7.

[3] The *De Animae Procreatione* presents us with an interesting contrast between tacit acceptance of Aristotelian positions and literal interpretation of Plato. At 1013d Plutarch argues against the believers in the logical construction, not the temporal creation of the world-soul (Xenocrates and Crantor reported by Eudorus of Alexandria). They had argued that Rest and Motion were derived from Same and Other. Plutarch answers that these are distinct Forms in the *Sophistes*. (He might have added that while Motion and Rest are mutually exclusive Forms, Same and Other are all-pervading.) Yet later we find him taking much the same line as Xenocrates himself concerning ἀμέριστον and μεριστόν. τὸ ἀμέριστον in the world-soul is equated with τὸ νοερόν, which is declared at 1024a *fin.* to be ἀκίνητον καὶ ἀπαθὲς καὶ περὶ τὴν ἀεὶ μένουσαν ἱδρυμένον οὐσίαν. Similarly τὸ μεριστόν is equated with the unordered world-soul (J. Helmer, *op. cit.* p. 32). Later at 1024c he declares that the fixed stars display Difference in Sameness, the planets Sameness in Difference.

Plato himself must be held responsible for some of this confusion. His description of the motion of the στρόβιλοι in the *Republic* (436d) is that they combine motion and rest. The static element in κυκλοφορία is stressed again at *Laws* x 893c 4, and the description of the motion of νοῦς at 897d sqq. (especially at 898a *fin.*) declares the relation of unity and sameness to rest in terms that recall all the description of the character of the Forms in the *Phaedo* and in the *Symposium*.

seems to be good reason for setting out the differences between Plato's doctrine in the *Timaeus* and the *Laws* and Aristotle's in a brief summary:

(i) Plato regards the activity of thought as a κίνησις, not in space and so not bodily, whose εἰκών is the rotation of a sphere. For Aristotle all κίνησις is ἐν τόπῳ: the functioning of νοῦς is ἐνέργεια and bears no resemblance to κυκλοφορία.

(ii) Plato regards κυκλοφορία as a possible motion of the four bodies: they are, indeed, as amenable to κυκλοφορία as to the random rectilinear motions caused by the shaking of the ὑποδοχή and they have no source of motion and rest in themselves. For Aristotle the bodies have natural motions to their places (and so to their forms) and since the four have rectilinear movement, a fifth moving naturally in a circle is required by the phenomena.

Plato, therefore, allows the physical figure of the sphere to colour his doctrine of psychic motion, though he had criticised the Eleatic assumptions so radically in the *Parmenides*. On the other hand, Aristotle's Pure Form never quite discards the physical aspect of the Parmenidean "sign" ἀκίνητον, and this fact obscures Plato's doctrine in all subsequent debate.

(d) Soul as a movent of body

Plato stays in the course of his refutation of the atheists in the tenth book of the *Laws* to enquire in what manner the soul of the sun guides its body. "Seeing, then, that a soul guides the sun, we shall not go far wrong in assigning to it one of three possible methods of doing this", says the Athenian; and he goes on to name these.[1]

Either it abides within the visible spherical body and guides it in all its ways in such manner, just as our soul within us takes us everywhere in our wanderings. Or it has provided itself with a body of fire or of a kind of air—as some would have it—and from somewhere outside forcibly propels its body with this body as its lever. Or thirdly without any body but by means of other supremely wonderful agencies it assists its body on its way.

Jaeger thinks that the third of these hypotheses represents the doctrine of the unmoved mover and that Aristotle learnt it in the

[1] *Laws* x 898 e 5 sqq.

Academy.[1] The second hypothesis he cannot assign to anyone definitely. But ποδηγεῖ is a strange phrase to describe an unconcerned πρῶτον κινοῦν ἀκίνητον: if Plato's own usage is any guide (as, for instance, *Politicus* 269c), it refers to an active concern by the motive power; the special point is simply that it cannot be thought to act in any physical sense on any point of the body. This point is therefore a tacit criticism of those who hold the second view of an intermediary movent in the form of a fiery or airy body. Plato seems to be saying that while the simple unscientific idea of the soul being "inside" the body is unsatisfactory, the attempts of "some" to mend it by introducing an intermediary tenuous body are unsatisfactory too, for the body is still only a body and the action a mere material impulsion (ὠθεῖ βίᾳ σώματι σῶμα) and therefore he prefers to leave the question a mystery. We must not be too ready to identify the τινές ourselves, but their doctrine bears a suspicious resemblance to the doctrine of σύμφυτον πνεῦμα of which Aristotle makes use in this connection in the *De Motu Animalium*.[2]

Such hints as the dialogues give us only bear out Plato's reticence on this point. The soul of the οὐρανός is "wrought throughout the whole and further wrapped about its body without" in the *Timaeus*, but in the *Laws* we are told as in the *Phaedo* that the soul eludes scientific investigation.[3] Of the manner of the action of the soul's energies upon the bodily processes we are told nothing definite. One can only point out that a technical term παραλαμβάνειν begins to be introduced to deal with the question. The Δημιουργός "took over" the visible chaos, or later τὰ πεφυκότα ἐξ ἀνάγκης;[4] the πρωτουργοὶ κινήσεις "take over" the δευτερουργοὶ κινήσεις.[5] This παραλαμβάνειν might be called a poetic metaphor, like μέθεξις: it is

[1] *Aristoteles*, Eng. tr. pp. 141 sqq.
[2] Ch. x; cf. *De Gen. Anim.* B 3, 736b 34 sqq.; *v. infr.* p. 91.
[3] *Tim.* 34 b, *Laws* 898 e *init.* Plutarch (*Platonicae Quaestiones*, 1002 c) takes these passages together but finds a physical "surrounding" of body by soul only in the former. Indeed his *quaestio* is concerned with harmonising the *Timaeus* with the *Laws* and the other dialogues. He must therefore take περιπεφυκέναι at 898 e 1 as we have taken it, to mean something like περιεῖναι or περιγεγονέναι—the soul survives (*i.e.* evades) all attempts to perceive it.
[4] *Tim.* 30a 2; *ib.* 68e 2.
[5] *Laws* x 897a 5.

juster to Plato to say that both expressions indicate the recognition of the existence of a specific problem, and that neither pretends to be a solution. Yet a consideration of Aristotle's treatment of the problem of the movement of body by soul reveals only too clearly how little Plato allowed himself to be concerned with it.

The psychophysical problem is perhaps the best illustration of Aristotle's attempt to be faithful to the principles of "natural philosophy" as he understood them and yet to follow Plato in excluding materialism. Unfortunately we have to infer his positive teaching very largely from those criticisms of Plato in which he wrestles for the measure of freedom and clarity he feels he must demand. The first passage of importance for us is one we have considered already—the criticism of the *Timaeus* in the first book of the *De Anima*. It is perhaps too facile to suggest that the whole issue turns on the use of the term ἐνέργεια in place of κίνησις for all activity which is not ἐν τόπῳ,[1] but the point that the soul cannot be said to move except *per accidens* in the body does seem laboured to excess. Indeed Aristotle seems at one point to assent to the proposition that the fact of movement of body by soul implies that soul as such has bodily movement—at least Simplicius can take him in this sense and fails to extract him from inconsistency in his comment.[2] But that this is no more than obscurity arising from

---

[1] So Hicks, Ar. *De Anima*, Intro. p. xxxvi. "What Plato calls 'movement' is familiar enough in Aristotle as 'energy' or 'activity'. If only Plato would say 'energy' there would seemingly be no room for objection. But in the tenth book of the *Laws*, the work of his old age, when he may be presumed to have had some acquaintance with the views of his disciple, Plato obdurately refused to say 'energy' and by his classification of the ten species of motion assimilated physical movement and change to the only activity which in his view had reality, the 'movement of thought'." This begs many questions—the word "assimilate" is particularly misleading. What is presumably intended is an insistence that Plato refuses to use any other word than κίνησις for the "tenth kind".

[2] ἔτι δὲ ἐπεὶ φαίνεται κινοῦσα κατὰ τὸ σῶμα, ταύτας εὔλογον κινεῖν τὰς κινήσεις ἃς καὶ αὐτὴ κινεῖται. εἰ δὲ τοῦτο, καὶ ἀντιστρέψασιν εἰπεῖν ἀληθές, A 3, 406a 30 sqq. The use of φαίνεται rather than δοκεῖ appears to imply assent by Aristotle. Simplicius *ad loc.* (*Comm.* p. 36, ll. 30 sqq.) sees the problem but evades it.

over-elaboration appears from Aristotle's criticism of Democritus later on, which he concludes with the remark ὅλως δὲ οὐχ οὕτω φαίνεται κινεῖν ἡ ψυχὴ τὸ ζῷον, ἀλλὰ διὰ προαιρέσεως τινὸς καὶ νοήσεως.[1] We conclude, then, from Aristotle's criticism of his predecessors in general and of the *Timaeus* in particular that he objects to the use of κίνησις for what is not ἐν τόπῳ and that προαίρεσις is that mode of the soul's ἐνέργεια which is to be regarded specifically as αἰτία κινήσεως.

This is confirmed when we come to consider Aristotle's positive doctrine in the third book of the *De Anima*. Here we meet the case of crucial importance, the locomotion of animals. For the manner of this is closely parallel to the motion of the πρῶτος οὐρανός as influenced by the First Mover. The importance of this comes out in the discussion of ὄρεξις and τὸ ὀρεκτὸν ἀγαθόν and the threefold classification of τὸ κινοῦν, τὸ κινοῦν καὶ κινούμενον and τὸ κινούμενον which is briefly recapitulated and assumed in *Metaphysics* Λ.[2] Here, of course, there are fascinating questions we must set aside. Why is ὄρεξις rather than intellectual contemplation the faculty that maintains the οὐρανός in being in so far as that being is expressed in its κυκλοφορία? Why does desire of the unmoved generate motion? There is reason for a horse to be "moved" by his food, but the πρῶτος οὐρανός can never for all its movement "get at" the object of its desire. "Strange too is that other thing that has been maintained," says Theophrastus in the fragment of his *Metaphysics*, "that the things that desire what is at rest do not imitate its immobility; for why does not, for those thinkers, the immobility of all other things follow on that of the First Mover?"[3] Is it some answer to these puzzles to say that Aristotle tried to explain motion in the macrocosm in the light of the manner of its generation in the microcosm at a point where he believed he could study it closely— in the communication of motion from the soul to the body of an animal moved by the sight of its food? Plato, as we have seen, had attempted, conversely, to explain the urges of the human and

---

[1] A 3, 406b 25.
[2] *De Anima* Γ 10, 433a 8 sqq.; *Metaph.* Λ 7, 1072a 18 sqq.
[3] Theophr. *Metaphysica* 7b 23 sqq., tr. Ross.

animal worlds by analogy with astronomical motions and the laws
governing the interfusion of the four bodies which depended on
these. But we must return to the actual account of the setting up
of motion in the horse by desire following on the sight of his food.

Taking the case of the moving of the tendons of the horse's leg
by the sight of food, we have according to the threefold classification
of the *De Anima*:

(*a*) τὸ κινοῦν ἀκίνητον—here the food. (In the case of sublunary
ἔμψυχα, τὸ ὀρεκτὸν ἀγαθόν is always proximately something perish-
able—unless, indeed, it be the λοξὸς κύκλος—but always ultimately
the immaterial πρῶτον κινοῦν.)

(*b*) τὸ κινοῦν καὶ κινούμενον—here the ὄρεξις.

(*c*) τὸ κινούμενον—here the tendon, and by it the leg and the horse.

Now of these the tendon is moved in space; it is the ὄργανον which
is, as Aristotle himself says, ἤδη σωματικόν.[1] But the ὄρεξις is
ἀσώματον and κινεῖσθαι should not be used of it if its use is to be
confined to what is ἐν τόπῳ. The inconsistency here probably
accounts for the disputed reading of the phrase immediately before:
καὶ ἡ ὄρεξις κίνησίς τίς ἐστιν ἢ ἐνέργεια.[2] This *saltus* from psychic
to spatial puts too great a strain on Aristotle's formula. But the
fact remains that he is concerned to track down and mark the exact
point at which the *saltus* occurs. This concern enters into his account of αἴσθησις in general and comes out in the statement that,
while the perceiving organ must be an extended magnitude, sensi-
tivity and sensing cannot be such—they are "a certain ratio and
power in a magnitude".[3] The difficulty of the *saltus*, however, is
increased in the case of ὄρεξις, where the percept is not simply so
much material for knowledge but also, and pre-eminently, a provoca-
tion to action.

Fortunately the *De Motu Animalium* and the *De Incessu Animalium*
survive[4] and give a positive and coherent account of what has to be

---

[1] 433 b 19.   [2] 433 b 17; *v.* Hicks *ad loc.*
[3] 424a 25 sqq. Oxford translation. See also Professor J. A. Smith's note
on the passage.
[4] Jaeger has recently given us a new edition of the text. Mr Farquharson's
(Oxford) translation and footnotes are very helpful.

collected from scattered references in the *De Anima*. In the *De Motu
Animalium* we find the problem set in the context of the teaching of
the *Physics*, the *Metaphysics* and the *De Anima*, with explicit recognition of the close relation to the doctrine of the First Mover which
we have already observed. As in all particular bodily motions there
must be that which moves without being moved (the elbow-joint,
for example, in a movement of the forearm), so there must be a point
at rest from which, and against which as *point d'appui*, all bodily
motions take place. Indeed the elbow-joint in our example is only
a relatively unmoved mover: there must be an absolutely unmoved
mover with a central organ in the body. "This something is the
soul, distinct from the spatial magnitude just described and yet
located therein."[1] Here is the scene of the transforming (if that be
the true description) of ὄρεξις into pushing and pulling of bodily
organs, and hence it comes about that the heart is abundantly
supplied with sinews.[2] Moreover, Aristotle brings in just at this
point an intermediary motive power, the σύμφυτον πνεῦμα, which
is physically generated from the blood but is "disposed to excite
movement and exert power by expansion and contraction".[3] The
province and effects of this are clearly defined, in contrast to the
later Stoic doctrine; and there seems no reason to suppose this
chapter of the *De Motu* spurious: it rather shows how devotedly
Aristotle tackled the psychophysical problem. We find an almost
similar use of this πνεῦμα as a "carrier" of the soul in the semen in
the account of generation. It appears as an active element distinct
from the secretion of bodily nutriment which exists purely in the
semen and impurely in the catamenia.[4] Here we are told that this
πνεῦμα is analogous to the fifth body of which the stars are composed, but it is an analogy of material constitution, not an analogy
of function. The πνεῦμα, like the matter of the stars, is not fire,

[1] 703 a 2 sqq.; *v.* Farquharson *ad loc.*
[2] *De Part. Anim.* Γ 4, 666b 13 sqq.   [3] 703a 19 sqq.
[4] *De Gen. Anim.* B 3, 736b 30 sqq. I am not sure whether the statement at
736 a 27 that the semen is only a secretion of the nutriment in process
of change is entirely in accord with the first book of the *De Generatione*
where the πνεῦμα seems to be regarded rather as a constituent of the
semen than as its proximate mover.

but may least untruthfully be conceived as a fiery air. There is no suggestion that the πνεῦμα in man has native circular motion. Rather it is an intermediary of the kind Plato discredits and denies to the soul of the sun in the *Laws*—"a body of fire or, as some would have it, a kind of air" with which, as with a lever, the soul propels the body from outside.[1] We may agree that in the case of the sun it is a doubtful expedient to introduce such a body, but its introduction into the problem of human and animal motion is not discredited so easily.

We have to consider also the indications that Aristotle realised more clearly than Plato did the difficulty of setting human and animal ἔμψυχα in an environment consisting (immediately, at least) of the four simple bodies. No doubt the difficulty was greater for him because he gave the simple bodies sources of motion and rest in themselves, which Plato did not, and so it must have been evident that the bodies of sublunary creatures possess motions of their own which are of necessity inhibited and controlled by the soul so long as they serve as its body. Taking the case of the horse once again, let us suppose he knocks down his stable door in his anxiety to get at his food. The horse (as σύνολον, soul and body) may be said to move (the wooden door) being moved (by his food-desiring soul). But though it is true that the motion arising in his tendons is more purpose-controlled and more subject to inhibition than the motion of the wooden door (which simply falls to the ground as it would have done had a chance fall of rock exerted equal pressure on it), yet the tendons are composed of ὁμοιομερῆ of earth and water which have their inherent motions imposed upon just as much as the door has, but imposed on over a longer period and according to an intelligible form and law. There is therefore an important distinction between ἔμψυχα (plants and animals alike) and both ἁπλᾶ σώματα on the one hand and οὐρανός on the other. Into a universe whose φύσις is fully expressed in its φορά—the circling spheres and the ἁπλᾶ σώματα moving each towards its form as it moves towards its place[2]—enters a plurality of sources of motion and rest exhibiting ἀλλοίωσις (which the heavens do not, though the simple bodies do)

[1] *Laws* x 898d *init.*; *v.* p. 86 *supr.*   [2] *De Caelo* Δ 3, 310a 33 sqq.

and in particular that very specialised form of ἀλλοίωσις called αὔξη which is peculiar to these souls. These ἀρχαὶ κινήσεως cannot be said to have a "matter" prepared to receive and express their activity in the sense that the πεμπτὸν σῶμα is ready for the celestial souls (assuming that there exist souls of the spheres which desire their Intelligences and move the σῶμα κυκλοφορητικόν). These ἀρχαί must organise the already moving simple bodies and this process seems to be compared by Aristotle in the *Physics*[1] to the principle of the lever, which "carries" a motion not inherent in itself at the behest of an ἀρχὴ κινήσεως. Unfortunately Aristotle is so concerned to point out in the passage in question (as in *De Anima* A 3) that the soul moves itself *per accidens* that he obscures the important points that the lever is not naturally capable of moving the weight and that there is evident in the case of the lever the "source of motion" which wields it and imparts a motion which is παρὰ φύσιν to the μοχλός as a σῶμα and to the σώματα it moves. The maintenance of this motion by the suppression or forcible transformation of the natural motions of the lever involves a strain, which eventually exhausts the ἀρχή, as is evident from a passage in the *De Caelo*[2] and by the clearest implication in a passage in *Metaphysics* Θ,[3] where we are told that the planets never weary (κάμνει) in their course. Simplicius's exposition of the meaning of κάμνειν in his comment on the *Physics* passage and his account of the general meaning of the *De Caelo* passage attest the doctrine of Aristotle beyond reasonable doubt.

Such was the wrestling of Plato's great pupil with the psychophysical problem. We have tried to show Plato's greater simplicity and his comparative freedom from primitive animism in his reduction of astronomical and sublunary kinds of motion to two—circular and rectilinear, caused by νοῦς and ἀνάγκη—thus avoiding a fifth body moving naturally in a circle and simple bodies each having its source of motion and rest in itself. But when we come to the realm of animals and plants and the temporary government of portions of the physical world by their souls it is to Aristotle we have

[1] *Phys.* Θ 8, 259a 20–b 30, esp. b 14 sqq.
[2] *De Caelo* B 6, 288b 15.   [3] Θ 8, 1050b 24 sqq.

to look for insight and originality. In comparison Plato merits the condemnation passed by his pupil on the Pythagoreans that according to their doctrines any soul could inhabit any body. Our consideration of Plato's debt to Alcmaeon has shown us how he bends contemporary medical knowledge into subservience to the implications of his recognition of literal περίοδοι in man's head analogous to the περίοδοι of the οὐρανός. Similarly on the psychophysical issue, Plato is hardly as explicit as Alcmaeon himself had been on the manner in which the brain furnishes the sensations. Certainly the marrow is a κύτος for the ψυχή, not a μοχλός by which it moves the body, though he does seem in his cursory treatment of generation to regard it as impregnated, as it were, with ψυχή which presses for release.[1] This may go back to Alcmaeon, who was more explicit and evidently far more interested in embryology than Plato.[2] At no point is the contrast with Aristotle more striking. αἴσθησις, moreover, seems to be regarded always as an assault and battery committed upon the ψυχή in its citadel in the brain. Sound is "a stroke given by the air through the ears to the brain and blood, continued to the soul" and hearing is "the motion due to this stroke, which begins in the head and ends in the quarter of the liver";[3] but this gives us little idea of what happens in the brain; moreover, there is difficulty in conceiving the physiological side of that perfect case of perception and judgment when the circle of the Other runs true and πίστεις βέβαιοι καὶ ἀληθεῖς are the result.[4]

In fine, Plato was so concerned to maintain that the bones and sinews of Socrates stayed in prison in Athens because of his soul's choice of the best, that he thought it unnecessary to enquire how his soul's decision, whether to go to Thebes or to sit where he was, communicated its command to those bones and those sinews.

For anyone who took a medical rather than a personal interest in the details of the death of Socrates, Plato would have felt the contempt Wordsworth had for

---

[1] *Tim.* 91 b; cf. 73 c, 74 e.   [2] Diels, *F. d. V.*[5] 24 A 13.

[3] *Tim.* 67 b; cf. 43 c, 81 d (notice how the soul is thought of in Orphic terms as distinct from the body and glad to leave it).

[4] *Tim.* 37 b; cf. 44 c.

One that would peep and botanise
Upon his mother's grave.[1]

Still less would he have concerned himself with the movements of
the cock sacrificed to Asclepius, for its soul had fallen from the
philosopher's estate in its witlessness. The one thing needful was to
see that soul was "senior to" body and controlled it: the varieties
of bodily movement were only interesting when the planetary
anomalies and the mingling of the so-called elements compelled
detailed study and classification.

[1] Wordsworth, *A Poet's Epitaph.*

CHAPTER VII

THE TEN KINDS OF MOTION

The significance of the refutation of the atheists which we find in the tenth book of the *Laws* is likely to remain a matter of dispute. Those who are interested in it as the first attempt in Europe at the formulation of a natural theology will tend to interpret the passage out of relation to the rest of Plato's thought, even if they escape the danger of reading back into it ideas of God which arose only in later times. On the other hand, when the Platonic scholar attempts the impossible but inevitable task of formulating a system of thought out of the dialogues themselves, he either underestimates the passage because it seems so dissonant both from the metaphysic of the *Republic* and the logical system of the *Sophistes* or else elevates it to an unnatural importance as crowning and superseding all that has gone before.

Into this latter danger any must come who treat the *Timaeus* in the way Burnet and Taylor have treated it. If Plato is restrained by limitations of his dramatic material in the *Timaeus* and cannot express himself freely on cosmological questions, the *Laws* does become the one authority for his later views on these questions, and this is presumably what Burnet means by claiming that the *Laws* is "strictly scientific".[1] On the other hand, if we take the *Timaeus* to be the essentially cosmological work and the *Laws* as sociological and political, the latter is not likely to give us anything new in the cosmological field, and, as for its theology, one must suspect any claim that something completely new arises here either —for is it not the cosmological argument which is the basis of the proof of divine existence? What appears to be scientific exegesis turns out on closer inspection to be "protreptic" elaboration of what can be found in the *Phaedrus* and the *Philebus* and, it must now be claimed, the *Timaeus*. This last claim requires detailed substantiation

[1] *Greek Philosophy, Thales to Plato*, p. 336.

and it seems possible to find it. We have at the beginning of the tenth book of the *Laws* a classification of motion into ten "kinds". Is this something new, or is it merely a convenient recapitulation of what has gone before in the *Timaeus*? We shall try to show that it is the latter, that, in fact, it reproduces the account of the motions that actually go on in the οὐρανός as we find them in the *Timaeus*, and more particularly, that the complex motions described at 893 e 6 sqq. are those described more fully in the account of the reciprocal transformations of the four chief bodies which we find at *Timaeus* 56d sqq. But we must consider the whole speech of the Athenian to Cleinias which begins at *Laws* 893 b:

Athenian. Come, then, and let this of all times be a time for calling on the aid of the Gods: with deepest devotion must they now be besought to aid, for it is to help us demonstrate their own existence. To this guiding-rope holding fast, let us enter upon the hazards of the argument before us. It seems to me that if I am taxed with questions such as these, there are the following answers which safely meet the questions which will be put. "Sir," one will ask me, "are all things at rest, nothing in motion, or is the contrary case true, or are some things in motion others at rest?" "Some in motion" (I reply) "others at rest." "Must it not be in space in some sense that the static rest and the moving move?" "Yes." "And some would move fixed in one place, others in a succession of places?" "Is it of moving things which have the power of being stationary at their centre that you speak", we shall reply, "when you say that they move in one place, like the revolution of so-called 'humming tops'?"[1] "Yes." "And we see that in such forms of revolution this kind of movement carries round the largest and the smallest circle at the same time and by distributing itself proportionally to small and great is itself smaller or greater in proportion. So it has become the source of marvels of all kinds, for it imparts at the same time to great and small slowness and swiftness in proportion to their size—a phenomenon one would have thought impossible." "Quite so." "Moreover, when you speak of things moved in a succession of places, you appear to be describing objects moving on continually from place to place, in some cases pivoting themselves at one point gliding along, in other cases rolling with changing pivotal

---

[1] Or "of wheels with fixed centres" (see p. 100 *infr.*). But λεγομένων may mean "so-called κύκλοι", which are in fact spherical "standing-tops".

points. And when on any occasion these several moving bodies clash with stationary objects they disintegrate; with other moving bodies meeting them from an opposite direction they coalesce, and midway between such clashing elements a new compound arises." "Yes, I grant that these things are as you describe them." "Moreover, bodies which receive additions are merely increased and those suffering division are merely lessened in bulk only when each remains the same 'element' as it was; in cases where it does not remain the same, addition and division are alike able to abolish it. Lastly there is coming-to-be universally;—under what conditions does it happen? When an origin achieves fluxion and arrives at the second dimension and from this at the third, and, arriving at the third dimension, goes on to become an object of perception. These are the changes and motions that attend all coming-into-being. Each thing is really what it is while it retains its construction, but when it is transformed into a body of another construction, its former being is completely destroyed. Maybe, friends, we have now numbered and classified all kinds of motion save two."

Cleinias. What are these two?

Athenian. Just the pair which it is the end of all our present examination to reveal.

Cleinias. I pray you to be plainer.

Athenian. We began to enquire in order to declare the dignity of soul, I think.

Cleinias. We did.

Athenian. Let us posit then one constant type of motion which can set other things in motion but cannot move itself; and a second constant type that is capable of imparting motion to other things under the forms of combination and disintegration, increase and diminution, coming-into-being and passing-away and is able to move itself as well.

Cleinias. Let these be the two kinds.

Athenian. Then the first of these constant types, that which moves objects but is altered itself from one form to another by the ulterior kind, we will make our ninth class; while for our tenth we may perhaps take that which moves itself as well as its object, accommodating itself to and exhibiting itself within all doing and being-done-to, and called, according to ultimate reality, the transforming and moving power among all things that exist.

Cleinias. Verily so.

The latter part of this passage gives us the key to the whole of it. Plato tells us (at 894 b 6) that the whole σκέψις is ψυχῆς ἕνεκα. After working out in detail the visible motions of the οὐρανός and of the four elemental bodies, he argues that all of them imply an ulterior "kind" of motion ἐναρμόττουσαν πᾶσιν μὲν ποιήμασι πᾶσιν δὲ παθήμασι, and the final point is made, with homiletic insistence, at 895 a: μῶν ἀρχή τις αὐτῶν ἔσται τῆς κινήσεως ἁπάσης ἄλλη πλὴν ἡ τῆς αὐτῆς αὐτὴν κινησάσης μεταβολή; All the motions but the tenth, therefore, are physical. It is true that ἁπλῆ γένεσις, which we shall find at 894a, is not physical in the ordinary sense of the word, but it would be dangerous to call it "mathematical", just as Taylor's use of the word "kinematical"[1] is dangerous if it implies no reference to actual physical motions going on in the οὐρανός all the time. In the sense that Plato's physics is geometrical, his dynamics is kinematical, but in no other sense is it so.

We need not spend time making out the ten kinds, or trouble ourselves with the various estimates that have been made. In any case the ninth is the genus of which the first eight are species, and the tenth is declared to be different in kind from the nine. If one feels the Pythagorean urge to bring the number up to ten one may perhaps add κυκλοφορία ἐν ἑνί and κυκλοφορία ἐν πολλοῖς (both gliding and rolling) to the six given at 894b *fin.*—combination and separation, growth and decrease, coming into being and passing away—or else one may group all κυκλοφορία together, ignore φθορά and find three motions involved in γένεσις: this, however, is far less satisfactory; for φθορά is brought in in the word ἀπόλλυται at the end of 893 e contrasted with φθίσις. We should keep, therefore, to Ast's enumeration. It remains only to comment on the passage in detail.

893 b *fin.*: τὰ μὲν κινεῖταί που, φήσω, τὰ δὲ μένει.

This sums up the compromise, or rather the synthesis, between Heracliteans and Eleatics achieved in the *Sophistes*.[2] The reference is to κίνησις and στάσις of physical objects, as we shall see. στάσις

---

[1] "Plato is describing the results of various combinations of motions from a purely kinematical, not a physical, point of view": A. E. Taylor, trans. p. 284 n. 5.

[2] It is also the view of "the natural man", from which the cobblers in the *Theaetetus* are unfortunately converted to Heracliteanism (*Theaet.* 180d—I owe the reference to Professor Cornford).

in nature occurs in two senses: (i) the constancy of the οὐρανός about its axis and of the heavenly bodies about theirs; (ii) the fact that a particular particle "remains" what it is (i.e. earth, fire, etc.), although it is in motion. Otherwise the Heracliteans are right about the physical world.

893 c *init.*: μῶν οὖν οὐκ ἐν χώρᾳ τινὶ τά τε ἑστῶτα ἕστηκεν καὶ τὰ κινούμενα κινεῖται;

Here τινί should perhaps be translated "in some sense". The "place" of ἁπλῆ γένεσις in its first two stages—the generations of line from origin and surface from line—is not the "place" common to the other motions and yet is thought of as closely related to this common "place". All the κινήσεις we are considering—all, that is, except the tenth kind—are what Aristotle also would term κινήσεις, for they are ἐν τόπῳ.

893 c 4: τὰ τὴν τῶν ἑστώτων ἐν μέσῳ λαμβάνοντα δύναμιν λέγεις, φήσομεν, ἐν ἑνὶ κινεῖσθαι, καθάπερ ἡ τῶν ἑστάναι λεγομένων κύκλων στρέφεται περιφορά;

The reason for the pride of place accorded to this kind of motion and the detailed exposition of it is, of course, because it is the motion of the οὐρανός itself, perfectly combining motion and rest;[1] the motion which is the εἰκών of νοῦς as Plato calls it later on, declaring it to be τῇ τοῦ νοῦ περιόδῳ πάντως ὡς δυνατὸν οἰκειοτάτην τε καὶ ὁμοίαν (897a *infr.*). The κύκλοι are either the στρόβιλοι of *Republic* IV 436d (for κύκλος appears to mean the same as σφαῖρα at 898a *infr.*; *v.* L. and S. *ad loc.*) or else the phrase means "wheels with centres fixed".

893 d 2: διὸ δὴ τῶν θαυμαστῶν ἁπάντων πηγὴ γέγονεν.

Taylor allows us to see a reference here to the orbits of the planets (trans. p. 284, n. 2). Actually there is nothing said about the ecliptic or the contrary direction of motion: ἐν ταύτῃ τῇ περιφορᾷ at c7 refers to the κύκλοι we have just considered. Yet the principle is valid for the Circle of the Other, and τῶν θαυμαστῶν ἁπάντων πηγή seems to refer to something actual, not to imaginary points on any radius of the οὐρανός, still less to a simple fact in kinematics. It was these θαυμαστά that took up so much of the time of the Academy.

[1] *V.* p. 97 n. 1 *supr.*

We have here in a summary form the language of *Timaeus* 39a and of *Laws* VII 822a, where the reference is to the double-motion astronomy: here, however, the distortion caused by the Circle of the Same is ignored and the character of the Circle of the Other (or for that matter, any such Circle) is considered ἁπλῶς. We see why Saturn is actually swiftest though considered slowest by men. These relative and proportionate "speeds and slownesses" are a basic element of the planetary motions. Cornford's statement, that only "the sun presents the motion of the Different unmodified", may be taken to mean that the sun exhibits the motion whose velocity is entirely determined by its distance from the centre along an imaginary radius of the Circle of the Other. In the case of each of the other planets there is some ἐναντία δύναμις, self-caused, which either accelerates or retards them in relation to the inherent velocity of the Circle of the Other at that point where each is placed. This does imply, however, that they would all finish their course in a solar year if their own δυνάμεις did not prevent it.

893d 6: τὰ δέ γε κινούμενα ἐν πολλοῖς... τότε μὲν ἔστιν ὅτε βάσιν ἑνὸς κεκτημένα κέντρου, τότε δὲ πλείονα τῷ περικυλινδεῖσθαι.

In passing from rotation to rectilinear motion we have to consider the forward movement of the sphere carried round in an orbit, exemplified in the motion of the fixed star "set in the mind of the highest" (*Tim.* 40a 5), or of the planet in its orbit, if one ignores in both cases proper rotation caused by their souls (which has really been dealt with already). Why Plato distinguishes gliding and rolling is not clear. The heavenly bodies rotate and glide but do not roll, for their axis is fixed. There may be a reference to lost theories of planetary motions or Plato may simply wish to give an exhaustive classification. This does not mean that rolling is not a "physical" motion: it is a physical possibility, even if not actualised in the planets. Indeed, it does occur in everyday life—it was the fate from which the gods saved the human head (*Tim.* 44d *fin.*). (Aristotle (*De Caelo* 290a) limits the possible motions of the stars to spinning and rolling, deciding against both: holding, as he did, that they are set in their spheres and carried round by them, he could not admit gliding even as a hypothesis.)

893 e *init.*: προστυγχάνοντα δ' ἑκάστοτε ἑκάστοις, τοῖς ἑστῶσι μὲν διασχίζεται, τοῖς δ' ἄλλοις ἐξ ἐναντίας ἀπαντῶσι καὶ φερομένοις εἰς ἓν γιγνόμενα, μέσα τε καὶ μεταξὺ τῶν τοιούτων συγκρίνεται.

We now pass from κυκλοφορία to rectilinear motions and from the combination of στάσις and κίνησις to sheer κίνησις. τοῖς ἑστῶσι μὲν διασχίζεται offers more difficulty than any other phrase for an interpretation of the passage as a summary of the *Timaeus* account of the interfusion of the four bodies. For even if we take ἑστῶσι of relative rest, as of any of the "elements" in its own region, it would seem that it is always the more mobile body which breaks down the less mobile. There is, it is true, the contrary case, which Cornford describes as the downward transformation, where fire is overpowered by much air, or both fire and air are quenched by water (*Tim.* 56e: Cornford, p. 226). These fire particles are called κινούμενα ἐν φερομένοις, however, and τοῖς ἑστῶσι διασχίζεται seems a strange description of their fate. Plato can hardly be ignoring this process, however, though his special reference here is probably to earth, which at *Timaeus* 55e (Cornford, p. 222) he calls ἀκινητοτάτη τῶν τεττάρων γενῶν καὶ τῶν σωμάτων πλαστικωτάτη. We hear little of this resistance of earth, for earth is but little mentioned in the account of the interfusion of the four bodies (Cornford, p. 245 n. 1): it is only when it "yields" that we are told of it, and even then it is not broken down into another kind. While no other kind can be broken down into it either, it must nevertheless be supposed to cause the kind of "thrusting" (ὠθεῖσθαι) which results in dissolution of its antagonists (διαλύεσθαι: *v. Tim.* 57b 5 sqq.; Cornford, pp. 227, 228) even more effectively than the other bodies. We can hardly suppose that the encounters which result in compounds with earth or the attacks which mould earth into its various forms (*Tim.* 60b sqq.) result in the escape of the attackers with impunity. τοῖς δ' ἄλλοις may imply a contrast between the three bodies based on the scalene triangle and the one based on the isosceles: it is, at any rate, to the "upward transformation" as Cornford calls it (pp. 224, 225; *Tim.* 56d) that the sentence seems to refer, for there could hardly be anything so special as a reference to the particles of intermediate size which give rise to odours (*Tim.* 66d; Cornford, pp. 273, 274) in so concise a summary. μέσα will therefore be air particles, intermediate between fire and water, the clashing opposites (τῶν τοιούτων). σύγκρισις is a general term, which we now go on to examine: for some σύγκρισις in the transformation process gives rise to a new "kind", other σύγκρισις only to the increase of an existing one. The position is negatively stated, however, and the distinction is rather made between two results (results rather than species) of διάκρισις—φθίσις and φθορά.

893 e 6: καὶ μὴν καὶ συγκρινόμενα μὲν αὐξάνεται διακρινόμενα δὲ φθίνει τότε, ὅταν ἡ καθεστηκυῖα ἑκάστων ἕξις διαμένῃ, μὴ μενούσης δέ, δι' ἀμφότερα ἀπόλλυται.

ἀμφότερα refers to σύγκρισις καὶ διάκρισις. ἀπόλλυται means that both can cause φθορά. σύγκρισις produces αὔξη in some cases, φθορά in others: διάκρισις produces φθίσις in some cases, φθορά in others. It depends in each case on the persistence of the καθεστηκυῖα ἕξις. If this persists, there is αὔξη (φθίσις); if not there is φθορά.

Our canon of interpretation at least gives us a clear meaning for καθεστηκυῖα ἕξις. England thinks it "a very obscure expression" which may refer to "conditions such as solid, liquid, gaseous". Taylor, on the other hand, would have it mean "kinematical configuration" (trans. p. 284 n. 5). We may combine the findings of both in a simplified explanation if we take it to mean the configuration of one of the four bodies, or more especially the three solid formations (pyramid, octahedron and icosahedron) of fire, air and water.[1] Earth will exhibit αὔξη and φθίσις in σύγκρισις and διάκρισις respectively: its καθεστηκυῖα ἕξις is unalterable. But between the other three bodies σύγκρισις may result in αὔξη (a) when a body returns to its own kind, for example when small portions of fire "battle through" a mass of water or air (or earth, for that matter) and "return home" (Tim. 57b 5), or (b) when a body "subdues" another and assimilates it. Fire is increased by the water and air it destroys, but so are the other two by the fire they conquer and "compel to stay with them" (Tim. 56d, 56e). Conversely, διάκρισις

---

[1] Sir W. D. Ross has pointed out to me the close connection between Plato's treatment of the καθεστηκυῖα ἕξις here and Aristotle's differentiation between γένεσις and αὔξησις etc.

results in φθίσις in the case of the fire which does "battle through" the other bodies in reduced quantity and is not assimilated: φθίσις also occurs to earth, as we have said. Air and water are less stable than the extremes and are liable to φθορά alike by σύγκρισις and διάκρισις, fire being their "destroyer". But fire can itself be destroyed in reprisal when its adversaries surround it in great force.

Professor Cornford points out, however,[1] that one must also consider as αὔξη and φθίσις the increase or decrease of bulk of the particle of an element, the passing from one grade of size to another described at *Timaeus* 57 c, d.[2] This can occur to air and water no less than to fire and earth: indeed Cornford adduces the case of melting metals which involves a kind of φθίσις of water.[3]

894 a *init.* : γίγνεται δὴ πάντων γένεσις ἡνίκ' ἂν τί πάθος ᾖ; δῆλον ὡς ὁπόταν ἀρχὴ λαβοῦσα αὔξην εἰς τὴν δευτέραν ἔλθῃ μετάβασιν, καὶ ἀπὸ ταύτης εἰς τὴν πλησίον, καὶ μέχρι τριῶν ἐλθοῦσα αἴσθησιν σχῇ τοῖς αἰσθανομένοις.

We now come to something that goes beyond the *Timaeus*. It must have puzzled the young men: perhaps it was intended as a holy Pythagorean mystery that could be put forth only in mysterious language. One may compare the language in which the "nuptial number" is couched in the eighth book of the *Republic*: there too the mathematical and physical senses of αὔξη are brought out[4] and we are reminded that for a Pythagorean the two senses cannot be as distinct as they are for us. But if the passage is mysterious to the young men it is entirely necessary and relevant to an account of the physical motions. We have just heard of φθορά, which occurs when water, for instance, becomes air. This is a complete account of φθορά—when the καθεστηκυῖα ἕξις is lost, Plato will say of an "element" διέφθαρται παντελῶς. But γένεσις calls for a deeper explanation. We have to probe below the visible collisions to account for what they have shown us. First of all we saw them as collisions and rebounds out of which either an aggregate or a compound might

[1] *Plato and Parmenides*, p. 198.
[2] Cornford, *Plato's Cosmology*, pp. 230 sqq.
[3] *Plato's Cosmology*, p. 250; *Plato and Parmenides*, p. 198.
[4] Cf. *Rep.* VIII 546 b: αὐξήσεις; *ib.* 546 c: τρὶς αὐξηθείς.

arise with a new direction of motion. We asked why one in one case (that of φθίσις) and the other in the other (that of φθορά)? This takes us back to the elementary triangles which compose the four bodies—the στοιχεῖα of the συλλαβαί (*Tim.* 48c). But to explain γένεσις—how the triangles come to be there—takes us further back, to the more remote principles (ἀρχαί) of *Timaeus* 53d. This ἀρχή is not the ἀρχή of *Phaedrus* 245c, the ἀρχή κινήσεως which is ψυχή, but the "origin" which is not a point but an indivisible line or ἀρχή γραμμῆς, in no dimension, as described by Aristotle at *Metaphysics* A 9, 992a 20. This ἀρχή "generates" the line, line generates surface, surface solid. This is the ἁπλῆ γένεσις in which Plato believes in defiance of the Parmenidean canon. In fact he goes back to the Pythagorean scheme by which the universe is constituted, but with his own modifications of it. Probably we are to understand a fourfold process here, with three αὔξαι. These are ἀρχή to line, line to surface, surface to solid, but there is probably a further step from geometrical solid to perceptible solid and ἐλθοῦσα αἴσθησιν σχῆ means "having come, proceeds to *acquire*". This does not seem altogether consistent with Theon of Smyrna's account of the "tetractys of growth" (p. 97 Hill.), which may very probably conserve helpful evidence on this matter. There we are told that the seed is analogous to the ἀρχή, growth in length to 2 and the line, growth in breadth to 3 and the surface, growth in thickness to 4 and the solid. Nor is it entirely consistent, either, with Aristotle's account in the *De Anima* (404b 18 sqq.) of what was contained ἐν τοῖς περὶ φιλοσοφίας, where αἴσθησις is *equated* with the solid as νοῦς with one, ἐπιστήμη with two and δόξα with three (the number of the surface). In any case the perceptible solid must come at the fourth remove from the ἀρχή—the only question is whether three previous αὔξαι are thought to leave a further stage necessary before perception is achieved.[1]

Two general points must be made concerning the passage. The first is that the processes are not logical and mathematical in the sense that they are other than physical. As we have already insisted

[1] I must refer to the full discussion of the evidence in Dr A. T. Nicol's (Mrs Markwick's) paper on "Indivisible Lines" in *Class. Quart.* vol. xxx.

they are motions that occur ἐν χώρᾳ τινί. Even the ἀρχή, which is in a sense "in no dimension", generates the line ἐν χώρᾳ τινί. Nor is this χώρα other than the χώρα of the ὑποδοχή or the τιθήνη γενέσεως. We have here the only explanation Plato gives us of the τρόπος τις δύσφραστος καὶ θαυμαστός by which the ὑποδοχή receives τὰ εἰσιόντα καὶ ἐξιόντα τῶν ὄντων ἀεὶ μιμήματα (*Tim.* 50c).

Secondly, it is insisted that "behind" these motions as behind all the others stands the "motion that moves itself" or ψυχή. We saw how Plutarch set himself to close this gap in Plato's exposition in the *Timaeus*,[1] but in closing it with ψυχή he was only bringing out the implications of the present passage. In fact the significance of the passage lies not so much in the nature of the "fluxions" intended (this mathematical or Pythagorean aspect of the matter came to occupy the Academy to the exclusion of everything else) as in Plato's insistence that the motions are "real" and "physical" (no less so than rolling and colliding) and are, like the others, outward effects of the working of ψυχή. None of the nine motions is conceivable without the tenth. It is ψυχή which presides over the copying out of the Forms upon the ὑποδοχή.

894a 5: μεταβάλλον μὲν οὖν οὕτω καὶ μετακινούμενον γίγνεται πᾶν. ἔστιν δὲ ὄντως ὁπόταν μένῃ, μεταβαλὸν δ᾿ εἰς ἄλλην ἕξιν διέφθαρται παντελῶς.

μὲν οὖν implies a summing-up of the whole passage. γίγνεται in a general reference seems strange after the special account of γένεσις we have just had; but the balance of the sentence requires us to take it so, for, as we have seen, διέφθαρται παντελῶς refers only to the passage from one καθεστηκυῖα ἕξις to another. Perhaps "these are the external changes (supervening on the primary changes we have considered) which attend coming-into-being" is the meaning of the phrase. ἔστιν δὲ ὄντως ὂν ὁπόταν μένῃ refers to the preservation of the ἕξις: so long as the fire remains fire it "truly is" fire. This attribution of being to natural entities follows on the recognition of γεγενημένη οὐσία in the *Philebus* and was foreshadowed, as we saw, in the second hypothesis of the second part of the *Parmenides*.[2]

[1] *De Animae Procr.* 1024c; *v.* Introduction, *supr.* p. xiv.
[2] *V.* ch. I *supr.* p. 14.

894 c 5: ἐναρμόττουσαν πᾶσιν μὲν ποιήμασι πᾶσιν δὲ παθήμασι.

This implies that all the ποιεῖν—πάσχειν that nature exhibits is classified under the eight kinds of motion now summarised as the ninth. Behind them all is ψυχή, operating through them all, and in them all. We have seen how Plato acknowledged Forms of all ποιήματα and all παθήματα at the end of his life according to the list in the seventh epistle (*Ep.* VII 342 d *fin.*; *v.* p. 20 *supr.*). Now we find soul animating the bodies which trace out the copies of these Forms. The soul is said to move κατά τε συγκρίσεις κ.τ.λ.... (894 b *supr.*).

But this does not involve panpsychism, for the πρωτουργοὶ κινήσεις are not directed simply to the governance of these δευτερ-ουργοὶ κινήσεις as their sole function. For then they would be ethically neutral. On the contrary, they use their powers according to their vision and choice of eternal, or at least supraphysical ends. These activities are τὰ ψυχῆς which are πρεσβύτερα τῶν τοῦ σώματος (896 c 5 to 897 b *infr.*).

In this last passage it is arguable that the *Laws* goes further than, or is at any rate more explicit than, the *Timaeus*, and this is perhaps to be expected, for we do not expect such developments in cosmology. Moreover, the difficulty of explaining how psychic "takes over" physical is so great (*v. supr.* p. 87), that Plato was not likely to lay stress on it in the *Timaeus*. But in all else, the *Laws* account gives us nothing but indistinct summarising or edifying elaboration of what we have learnt already about κίνησις, of bodies and of ψυχή; and the attempt to exalt the validity of the *Laws* for Plato's "later doctrine" to the disparagement of the *Timaeus* seems to have but little justification.[1]

[1] I am deeply indebted to Professor Cornford's help and suggestion in the working out of the details of this passage. Without his *Timaeus* commentary, as will be seen, it could not have been carried through.

CHAPTER VIII

THE ULTIMATE ΑΡΧΗ ΚΙΝΗΣΕΩΣ IN PLATO

We have sought to show that Plato recognised what Aristotle later called the αἰτία ἡ ἀρχὴ κινήσεως and we have been content to describe this αἰτία as ψυχή—the motion that moves itself, as Plato himself defines it in the tenth book of the *Laws*. But we have already had reason to regard this discussion in the *Laws* as popular rather than scientific and to look to the more esoteric *Timaeus* for clearer evidence of Plato's real view. We must now do the same in an attempt to define more exactly the ultimate ἀρχὴ κινήσεως in Plato. We shall see how an unduly high valuation of *Laws* x, together with a realisation of the difficulties it raises, may have led to an abandonment of Plato's "theology"[1] as no more than μῦθος, an abandonment which is against the evidence of the later dialogues.

The question that Plato in *Laws* x neither answers nor encourages young men to ask is whether the ultimate ἀρχὴ κινήσεως is ψυχή or νοῦς. An answer can be given from the *Timaeus* if the general interpretation of the dialogue already attempted be accepted. This answer would be that of any κίνησις within the οὐρανός the proximate αἰτία is one or more ψυχαί. But all ψυχαί which originate bodily motions are derived or (lest we seem to forestall neo-Platonism by this expression) "generated". There is an ultimate *causa causarum* called in the *Timaeus* δημιουργός and πατήρ. The δημιουργός is not to be confused with the αὐτόζῳον, which is the object of his contemplation.[2] He may be said to perform both the functions which all thinkers ascribed to the soul according to Aristotle. He knows the Forms (and is distinct from what he knows) and he initiates motion by creating the world-soul. Yet this creation is, even if we take the myths quite literally, a creation in the sense of introducing the organs or factors whereby order may be imposed upon chaos.

[1] In the sense of the τύποι περὶ θεολογίας of *Rep.* 379 b.
[2] Cornford, *Plato's Cosmology*, pp. 40, 41.

Forms, ψυχὴ ἀόριστος, and ὑποδοχή all exist apart from the δημιουργός, and each is a *sine qua non* of his demiurgic activity.

We must enquire from the dialogues themselves what is meant by describing the ultimate ἀρχὴ κινήσεως as δημιουργός and as πατήρ. Under these two titles the others may be subsumed and so may the verbs used to describe his activity. δημιουργός is easier to trace through the earlier dialogues. The λόγοι ἐπακτικοί of Socrates were largely based on the analogy of the arts. Socrates had found the καλοὶ δημιουργοί truly wise in their several realms, even if they paraded a false wisdom in ultimate matters on the strength of this. A τέχνη is other than a τριβή, we are told in the *Gorgias*, and we proceed to the generalisation that the τεχνίτης or δημιουργός is a bringer of τάξις and κόσμος according to an ordered scale—here we join forces with the Pythagorean ἁρμονία doctrine.[1] The idea is developed in the *Cratylus*, where we are told that the νομοθέτης alone is competent to manufacture names, for he alone understands their real nature.[2] Here we come very close to the φύλαξ of the *Republic*, who rules the city in accordance with his vision of the Good.[3] It is only in the *Sophistes*, however, that we find a δημιουργῶν θεός whose activity is a form of ποιητική.[4] His

---

[1] Cf. *Gorgias* 503 e *fin.*: οἶον εἰ βούλει ἰδεῖν τοὺς ζωγράφους, τοὺς οἰκοδόμους, τοὺς ναυπηγούς, τοὺς ἄλλους πάντας δημιουργούς, ὅντινα βούλει αὐτῶν, ὡς εἰς τάξιν τινὰ ἕκαστος ἕκαστον τίθησιν ὃ ἂν τιθῇ καὶ προσαναγκάζει τὸ ἕτερον τῷ ἑτέρῳ πρέπον τε εἶναι καὶ ἁρμόττειν, ἕως ἂν τὸ ἅπαν συστήσηται τεταγμένον τε καὶ κεκοσμημένον πρᾶγμα.

[2] *Crat.* 390 d. The suggestion that the νομοθέτης ought to have a διαλεκτικὸς ἀνήρ for his ἐπιστάτης hints that names are not the true φύσις and therefore not the primary concern of the philosopher; but the way the δημιουργὸς ὀνομάτων acts would be the way the διαλεκτικός acts in his higher sphere.

[3] The actual word δημιουργός is not common, but the idea is all-pervading. Mr M. B. Foster's question "quis custodes custodiet?" (*The Political Philosophies of Plato and Hegel*, esp. ch. 1) is perhaps to be answered by saying that the Guardian governs himself κατὰ συμβεβηκός as guardian but ἁπλῶς as philosopher. *Republic* 500 d seems to attest this: ἂν οὖν τις, εἶπον αὐτῷ, ἀνάγκη γένηται ἃ ἐκεῖ ὁρᾷ μελετῆσαι εἰς ἀνθρώπων ἤθη καὶ ἰδίᾳ καὶ δημοσίᾳ τιθέναι καὶ μὴ μόνον ἑαυτὸν πλάττειν, ἆρα κακὸν δημιουργὸν αὐτὸν οἴει γενήσεσθαι σωφροσύνης τε καὶ δικαιοσύνης καὶ συμπάσης τῆς δημοτικῆς ἀρέτης;

[4] *Sophistes* 265 b 8 sqq.

work is contrasted with that of φύσις ἄνευ διανοίας. This passage prepares us for the close similarities we have already noticed between the *Politicus* myth, the *Philebus* (which is generally allowed not to be "mythical" in any sense) and the *Timaeus*. Purposeful and intelligent information of a given matter with a copy of a given form is the activity intended by δημιουργεῖν and none of the passages justifies the identification of the δημιουργός with the model which he copies.

It is the other title, πατήρ, which is almost new[1] and entirely new in its special sense in the *Timaeus*. We must put aside any comparison with the Aristotelian doctrine of generation,[2] for the title δημιουργός covers the activity of informing matter and πατήρ stands for something more. God is the "father" of the lesser gods, of the soul of the world, the souls of the stars and the souls of the planets. He stands in a less direct relation to human, animal and vegetable souls.

Here we have to define, necessarily very dogmatically, our attitude to the mythical elements of the dialogue.[3] M. Frutiger has made a clear and valuable distinction between the two types of myth which are to be found, sometimes intertwined, in the *Timaeus* creation-story. We have on the one hand the physics, on the other the cosmogony.[4] It is the latter with which we are now concerned. We have already distinguished[5] the εἰκὼς μῦθος of the physics from the μῦθος which strives to become λόγος—the μῦθος which is potentially λόγος since it concerns ὄντως ὄντα. Such is the μῦθος concerning the δημιουργός: the ultimate ἀρχὴ κινήσεως, though hard to find and never to be declared to the majority of men, is as real as the Forms. But we cannot follow Frutiger in regarding the creation

---

[1] It occurred in the *Politicus* myth—at *Polit.* 273 b.
[2] I disagree here with Mr Foster (*Mind*, XLIV, pp. 459 sqq.).
[3] We are not concerned with the Atlantis myth.
[4] Perceval Frutiger, *Les mythes de Platon* (Paris, 1930), p. 190: "Nous avons donc affaire à des mythes de l'espèce que nous appelons génético-symbolique, ou plus brièvement génétique, parce que le devenir qui s'y trouve dessiné correspond à un ordre logique et non pas à une succession temporelle": *ib.* p. 191.
[5] Introduction, *supr.* p. xv.

story as only a logical analysis put for the sake of clarity in the form of a synthesis. It may not be a literal account of what happened in the past, but it is a description of the actual process of the world in which we live and it purports to tell the interrelation of those supraphysical powers whose activities lie behind visible bodily motions.

There is no *creatio ex nihilo*. The pre-cosmic πλανωμένη αἰτία and the ἴχνη of the four bodies are as ultimate as the Δημιουργός. His power to "persuade" alone entitles him to "seniority". For we may not suppose that the πλανωμένη αἰτία acts only after the creation of the world-soul. What Plutarch says in the *De Animae Procreatione* cannot be so easily set aside. One cannot dismiss the doctrine of a literal creation of the formed universe in time by quoting the saying that time came into being with the universe. This does not imply that there was no duration before the creation of the formed universe. χρόνος is the image of eternity moving *according to number*: it is the πέρας imposed upon an ἄπειρον of duration. With the undetermined chaos there was an undetermined duration and this was the reign of the πλανωμένη αἰτία. If this can be accepted, we may *then* go on to argue that all these factors (πλανωμένη αἰτία, unformed "traces" of the four bodies and undetermined duration) are not to be taken literally but describe a constant undercurrent in the life of the existing world. But we cannot reach such a conclusion by taking the sentence χρόνος δ' οὖν μετ' οὐρανοῦ γέγονεν out of its context as ruling out a creation ποτέ because it rules out a creation ἐν χρόνῳ.[1]

Aristotle claims that he is the first to teach that the οὐρανός never had a beginning in time.[2] This follows, no doubt, from his literal view of the *Timaeus*. But it would still be true on our interpretation

[1] I have found Mr Gregory Vlastos's article on "The Disorderly Motion in the *Timaios*" (*Class. Quart.* vol. XXXIII) very helpful, but I venture to charge him with needless inconsistency in arguing that the pre-cosmic chaos cannot be moved by soul because God "creates" the world-soul. I am not convinced by his appeal to *Tim.* 57e, where κίνησις is said to be found under conditions of ἀνωμαλότης. This is only the "bodily" aspect of the σεισμός wrought by ἀνάγκη.

[2] *De Caelo* A 10, 279 b 12.

that he was the first to declare the οὐρανός to be ἀγένητος. For the *Timaeus* gives it a derived and dependent being and makes it not inherently imperishable. So it is with the subordinate gods and so also with stars and planets.

To call the ultimate ἀρχὴ κινήσεως πατήρ as well as δημιουργός implies, therefore, a development of the earlier view that ψυχή without qualification is such an ἀρχή. Commentators have been slow to admit that ψυχή is generated (except διδασκαλίας χάριν) because of the apparent contradiction of the *Phaedrus* and of *Laws* x[1] which such a view seems to imply. We have seen how Plutarch attempted to reconcile the *Phaedrus* and the *Timaeus* and to vindicate Plato from the charge of being a "drunken sophist" by declaring the pre-cosmic world-soul to be ungenerated. That this pre-cosmic soul is there to receive the ordering creative activity of the δημιουργός seems indeed to be the teaching of the *Timaeus*, as we have already suggested. But this is not what Plato meant in the *Phaedrus*. There he was affirming that the existing process of the universe postulated an ungenerated and imperishable ἀρχή. He was content to name it ψυχή. But in the *Sophistes* we find the claim for "perfect reality" made for κίνησις καὶ ζωὴ καὶ ψυχὴ καὶ φρόνησις. Then the Eleatic stranger continues:

"But are we to say that (the totality of the real) possesses mind but yet does not possess life?"
"Impossible."
"But if we say it contains them both, can we deny that it has them resident in soul?"
"How else could it have them?"[2]

This idea that νοῦς must be ἐν ψυχῇ is reiterated in the *Philebus*[3] and *Timaeus*.[4] Professor Hackforth interprets these passages as meaning that νοῦς in the created universe always requires ψυχή as a means whereby it may transmit its rational effects to the bodily

---

[1] Yet *Laws* x speaks of the ψυχή as γεγενημένη at 892c; cf. 892a, 896a. The crucial passage in the *Laws* is XII 967d. On this see Hackforth, art. "Plato's Theism", *Class. Quart.* XXX, p. 5.
[2] *Sophistes* 249a.   [3] *Philebus* 30c.
[4] *Timaeus* 30b.

realm. He quotes Proclus's commentary on the *Timaeus* in support of this contention.[1] On this view God is pure νοῦς rather than an ἀρίστη ψυχή, and we approach Aristotle's doctrine of the unmoved mover, but with a closer relation to the universe. One may best state Hackforth's conclusion in his own words:

Aristotle's God is external to the universe which depends on him and is connected with it only inasmuch as he is the object of its desire (ὡς ἐρώμενον). Plato's God is external too, in the sense that he is the perfect spiritual activity implied by, but nowhere fully revealed in, the Universe: at the same time he is immanent, in the sense that the life of the Universe is *his* life just because his activity is necessarily (unlike that of Aristotle's God) one that goes outside himself, is necessarily a projection of himself. To identify him with ψυχή would be to deny his transcendence or externality, since ψυχή is a principle operative only in the realm of κίνησις and γένεσις: and thereby to deny his perfection, since perfection does not and cannot belong to κίνησις and γένεσις.

This solution, attractive as it is, is perhaps rather too Aristotelian. To take the last words first, we have seen reason to believe that Plato did think of a kind of κίνησις of νοῦς, which he called κίνησις though κυκλοφορία was only the εἰκών of it. Perfection can belong to κίνησις. But perfection cannot belong to γένεσις, and we return to the question of the "generated" soul. Here it seems that Plato has given closer attention to the facts since he enunciated the general statement in the *Phaedrus* that there must be an ungenerated ἀρχή κινήσεως in order that becoming may not fail. We were in doubt there whether ψυχὴ πᾶσα means "all soul" or "every soul".[2] The question cannot have escaped Plato himself. Even if individual souls were immortal, their "cycle" of existence was not one which offered a certain hope that the orderly cosmos would never collapse. Yet there must be an ultimate ἀρχή to give real basis for this hope. By the time of the *Politicus* myth we seem to reach the insight that the soul of the universe is not in itself a reliable guarantee of the perfect order: it contains within itself σύμφυτος ἐπιθυμία which has to be

---

[1] οὐχ ὅτι δεῖται τῆς ψυχῆς ὁ νοῦς... ἀλλ' ὅτι τὰ σώματα δεῖται τῆς ψυχῆς εἰ μέλλοι νοῦ καθέξειν, Procl. *In Tim.* 1 402 (Diels) quoted by Hackforth, art. "Plato's Theism", *Class. Quart.* XXX, p. 8.

[2] *Phaedrus* 246b; *v.* p. 3 n. 1 *supr.*

corrected by God, the leader of all things that move. So it would seem that the place of the δημιουργὸς καὶ πατήρ became fixed. He is the ultimate ἀρχή: lesser gods, οὐρανός and star and planet souls are only subordinate ἀρχαί, and men, animals and plants are more subordinate still. Each soul may be said to be a δημιουργός, albeit a φαῦλος δημιουργός in so far as it fails to achieve τάξις and κόσμος in that part of the bodily realm which it controls. But only God is δημιουργός and πατήρ. In him alone is the perfection which the rest gain or miss according to their moral insight.[1] He is above time, in the sense that there are no "instants" in his life. Of other embodied souls this cannot be said, but the statement that they can be dissolved only at God's bidding[2] implies for them a kind of "new creation every instant" by the Father, to borrow the language of Descartes in the *Third Meditation*.

But does it follow that "Artificer" and "Father" are only names for νοῦς and that God is not a ψυχή? There seem two main reasons against this conclusion. The first is that νοῦς and ἄνοια seem to be factors governing ψυχαί, but the ψυχαί are the existent units in which they operate. In the case of the οὐρανός the αἰτίαι, νοῦς and ἀνάγκη, are, once again, operant factors, but the ψυχή is the real existent in which they are manifested. It seems, therefore, that while, of course, God is not ψυχὴ ἐν σώματι and is underived and initiates no direct bodily movement, he may yet be an ἀρίστη ψυχή, dominated entirely by νοῦς in a way no created ψυχή can be. This is really bound up with the other consideration, arising from the ethics which is so fused with cosmology and metaphysics in the later dialogues. Here the "impersonality" of pure νοῦς does seem to be a grave objection. No doubt Plato's God need not be "personal"

---

[1] The πλάνη of souls in error may be described in lines by one of the Wesleys:

> Upright both in thought and will
> We by our God were made,
> But we turned from good to ill
> And o'er the creature strayed,
> Multiplied our wandering thought
> Which first was fixed on God alone,
> In ten thousand objects sought
> The bliss we lost in one.

[2] ἄλυτα ἐμοῦ γε μὴ ἐθέλοντος, *Tim.* 41 a *fin.*

to perform his metaphysical office of being the ultimate ἀρχὴ κινήσεως. No doubt there is danger of introducing an irrelevant Christian conception of "personality" and rashness in translating ψυχή as "personality". But we may and should consider Plato's own theological predilections. The old Socratic morality and the Socratic piety are living factors in the fusion of ethics and metaphysics. To say that Plato's God is an ἀρίστη ψυχή is not to say that he is an omnipotent creator. Plato's ethics posit a being unfailingly good, in this distinct from lesser souls who can do evil.[1]

We are left, then, with an ἀγαθὸς δημιουργός and τὸ ἀγαθόν as ultimates. Plato was as capable as we are of realising that ἀγαθός and ἀγαθόν are parts of the same word, but his Socratic piety and his recognition of the difficulty of accounting for κίνησις by the static ἀγαθόν led him to believe in the masculine, as masculine, as much as in the neuter. To believe in either is, ultimately, an act of religious faith. To assert that Plato believed in both is to claim that he believed in an ultimate ἀρχὴ κινήσεως distinct from the Form of the Good. The coalescence of these ultimates never occurred in Plato's own thought, so far as that thought is recoverable for us. The very fact that such coalescence[2] was later on held necessary makes it the more important to maintain the distinction in Plato himself. In so doing we defend Plato against one of Aristotle's most searching criticisms, and we also come to see how the αἰτίας ζήτησις of the young Socrates described in the *Phaedo* occupied Plato himself to the end of his days.

[1] The problems of sinlessness could not arise for Plato in their later forms. His persistent acceptance of the Socratic canon οὐδεὶς ἑκὼν ἁμαρτάνει precluded their arising for him. God makes no involuntary mistakes.

[2] Perhaps Plato's search for the Ultimate would have led him away from the Idea of the Good as conceived in *Republic* VI rather than to any "coalescence" of the Good with God. Just as in the *Sophistes* he expressed dissatisfaction with static Forms devoid of life and thought and asserted that True Being was greater than they, so he might have come to insist that the Ultimate "beyond Being" must be the Origin of souls as well as of Forms. The difficulty for us is that he never reached a dialectic related to this Ultimate in the way the dialectic of *Republic* VII is related to the Idea of the Good. We can only trace his thought as far as it goes and try to distinguish clearly what Plato began from what his followers strove to complete.

BIBLIOGRAPHY

Standard works and translations are omitted from the bibliography. The portions of Simplicius's *Commentaries* on Aristotle that have been found particularly relevant have been noted in the Index of Passages. They come from Volumes 7, 9, 10 and 11 of the Berlin Edition.

The following abbreviations are used:

A.G.P. Archiv für Geschichte der Philosophie (quoted in the "*alte Folge*").
J.P. Journal of Philology.
Cl. Qu. Classical Quarterly.
F.d.V. in the footnotes refers to Kranz's fifth edition of Diels's *Fragmente der Vorsokratiker*, and *D.G.* to *Doxographi Graeci.*

I. On the *Timaeus*:

Commentaries consulted include Chalcidius (ed. Wrobel, Lipsiae, 1876), Proclus (ed. Diehl, Lipsiae, 1903–1906), Martin, Archer-Hind, Apelt, Rivaud (Budé series), Taylor, Cornford.

II. On κίνησις:

H. C. BALDRY. "Embryological Analogies in pre-Socratic Cosmogony." *Cl. Qu.* XXVI, pp. 27–34.

J. B. BURY. "Questions connected with Plato's *Phaidros*." *J.P.* xv, pp. 80–85.

W. A. HEIDEL. "Qualitative Change in pre-Socratic Cosmology." *A.G.P.* XIX, pp. 333–379.

LUIGIA STELLA. *Importanza di Alcmeone nella storia del pensiero greco,* in *Rendiconti della Reale Accademia Nazionale dei Lincei*, Ser. VI, vol. VIII, fasc. IV.

J. STENZEL. *Über zwei Begriffe der platonischen Mystik,* ζῷον *und* κίνησις. Breslau, 1914.

G. VLASTOS. "The Disorderly Motion in the *Timaeus.*" *Cl. Qu.* XXXIII, pp. 71–83.

J. M. WATSON. *Aristotle's Criticisms of Plato.* Oxford, 1909.

III. On Plato's Cosmology in general:

F. M. CORNFORD. *The Invention of Space.* Oxford, 1936. (Essays in honour of Gilbert Murray.)

M. B. Foster. "Christian Theology and Modern Science of Nature."
   Mind, XLIV, pp. 439–466, XLV, pp. 1–27.
R. Hackforth. "Plato's theism." Cl. Qu. XXX, pp. 4–9.
H. Jackson. "Plato's later theory of Ideas." J.P. x, pp. 253–298.
—— "Plato, Cratylus, cc. 42–44", in Cambridge Praelections, 1906.
T. H. Martin. "Hypothèse astronomique de Pythagore." Bullettino di
   Bibliografia e di Storia delle scienze matematiche e fisiche, V (1872),
   pp. 99–126.
N. R. Murphy. "The Δεύτερος Πλοῦς in the Phaedo." Cl. Qu. XXX,
   pp. 40–47.
A. T. Nicol. "Indivisible Lines." Cl. Qu. XXX, pp. 120–126.
G. Rodier. "Sur l'évolution de la dialectique de Platon." Année
   Philosophique, XVI, pp. 49–73.
L. Rougier. "La correspondance des Genres du Sophiste, du Philèbe
   et du Timée." A.G.P. XXVIII, pp. 305–334.
J. Tate. "On Plato, Laws 889 c d." Cl. Qu. XXX, pp. 48–54.
A. E. Taylor. "The 'Polytheism' of Plato: an Apologia." Mind,
   XLVII, pp. 180–199. (See also Cornford, ib. pp. 321–330.)
—— "The Decline and Fall of the State in Republic VIII." Mind,
   XLVIII, pp. 23–38.
M. Wellmann. "Eine pythagoreische Urkunde des IV Jahrhunderts v.
   Chr." Hermes, XIV, pp. 225–248.
Konrat Ziegler. "Menschen- und Weltenwerden." Neue Jahrbücher
   für das klassische Altertum, XXXI, pp. 529–573.

IV. On Plutarch, De Animae Procreatione in Timaeo:

J. Helmer. Zu Plutarch's De Animae Procreatione in Timaeo; ein Beitrag
   zum Verständnis des Platon-Deuters Plutarchs. Würzburg, 1937.
P. Thévenaz. L'âme du monde, le devenir et la matière chez Plutarque.
   Paris, 1938.

INDEX OF PASSAGES

For Plato, the references are given first to passages in the *Timaeus* and then the assumed chronological order is followed. For the Pre-Socratics, fragments are quoted according to their number in the 5th edition of Diels, *Fragmente der Vorsokratiker* (unless otherwise stated).

F.d.V. = Diels, *Fragmente der Vorsokratiker*.
D.G. = Diels, *Doxographi Graeci*.

Printed in the United States
By Bookmasters